EXCLUSIVE BY-PATH

EXCLUSIVE BY-PATH

The Autobiography of a Pilgrim

by

CHRISTINE WOOD

Now, a little before them, there was on the left hand side of the road a meadow, and a stile to go over into it, and that meadow is called By-path Meadow.—Pilgrim's Progress

Published by

ARTHUR JAMES LIMITED

THE DRIFT, EVESHAM, WORCS.

WR11 4NW

First Edition 1976

© Christine Wood 1976

All rights reserved by the publishers
Arthur James Limited, The Drift, Greenhill Park Road,
Evesham, Worcs., WR11 4NW, England

ISBN 0 85305 183 6

MADE AND PRINTED IN GREAT BRITAIN BY PURNELL AND SONS, LTD.
PAULTON (AVON) AND LONDON

DEDICATION

In Loving Memory of Geoffrey,
who led me back to where
the good way is.

THE GOOD WAY

Thus says the Lord: "Stand by the roads, and look, and ask for the ancient paths, where the good way is; and walk in it, and find rest for your souls"—Jeremiah 6: 16 R.S.V.

ACKNOWLEDGMENTS

I WISH to acknowledge the kind permission given by the following publishers and authors to quote from their works:

Chorus from the hymn beginning, *Walking with Jesus, by His side I'll stay . . .*—The Charles M. Alexander Copyrights Trust (Ch. 3)

A Sprig of Rosemary by Beryl Netherclift (Ch. 8)

Extract from *The House that Died*—Victory Press Ltd. (Ch. 1)

Extract from *The Amazing Results of Positive Thinking* by Norman Vincent Peale—Worlds Work Ltd. (Ch. 14)

Walking in the King's Highway—Copyright Rodeheaver Co., U.S.A. (Ch. 14)

———————

FOREWORD

by

the Rev. Canon Alan Neech,

General Secretary of the Bible Churchmen's Missionary Society

THIS LITTLE BOOK evokes pity, laughter, indignation and admiration. But in writing this moving account of her life, Christine Wood had a different purpose altogether. She wanted to share with as many as possible her witness to a loving Heavenly Father who sustains, guides and gives courage bravely to face life even when things are desperately hard.

The story is easily read, for it is both well-written and of great interest, but the inspiration of it will be long enduring.

Unhappiness, bewilderment, loneliness and bereavement at an early age are all found here, as well as excitement and the enjoyment of earth's abundant beauties. When you have read it you will at once think of several persons to whom you will want to pass it on.

The author is still in early middle age. At some time she must write a sequel.

Ealing, London, 1975   CANON ALAN NEECH

PREFACE

I THINK of life as a pilgrimage. The journey begins in childhood, passing through the turbulent teens into maturity. In our more thoughtful moments we wonder what life is all about. We try to discover ourselves and our reason for living. Somewhere along the way many of us search for the truth and happy are we if we find it. But if we are not careful the search can take us into some strange places.

My search led me into a close, fanatical religious sect. It was a kind of love-hate relationship. I loved many of the Exclusive folk with whom I walked and yet I hated and feared the harsh legal system that bound and enslaved us.

This is the story of my pilgrimage—how I wandered off the King's highway into a by-path from which it was extremely hard to retrace my steps. This book is also my testimony to the faithfulness of a loving Heavenly Father Who bears with our waywardness and ignorance and patiently waits until we are willing to be led back to His highway of love, peace and sunshine.

CHRISTINE WOOD

Surrey, 1975

CONTENTS

Chapter 1

A PILGRIMAGE BEGINS

CRASH! Another tile shattered as it hit the concrete path.

"How sad, that lovely old house is dying," I said to my husband.

I referred to the mellow-bricked house beyond the trees at the end of our garden. Already the gabled chimneys and gargoyles had gone. Now the demolishers attacked the roof.

"Soon it will be no more than a memory to those who've known and loved it," I grieved.

"Don't be so gloomy," Geoffrey said, turning over in bed. "Write a book about a house that died and give it a happy ending. Then you won't mind about their pulling that old place down."

No one could equal my husband for positive, practical advice, even when he was half asleep. And so a book was born amid the creak and groan of prised-up rafters. The timing was perfect. Our summer holiday began that day, which meant that I would have plenty of time to devote to my brain-child.

We had dreadful weather, yet that was one of our happiest holidays. We drove eagerly to our Brixham flat overlooking a quaint Devon harbour. When it rained (as it did most of the time) we worked on the book. While I wrote, Geoffrey studied nineteenth-century fashions, making notes on the various styles. Some Victorian

15

gowns were to be discovered in my "dying house" and my descriptions would have to be accurate.

Although this was a children's book, death wove itself into the fabric of the story, not gloomily but in a way that would, I hoped, be helpful and comforting. Basically the book was fun to write, except the chapter that touched on the death of the heroine's mother. I felt compelled to pray before writing that chapter.

"Dear God," I said, "it's as if You want me to define clearly what I believe about death and bereavement. Why?"

God did show me why, but not then. Instead He gave me the energy to finish the book quickly.

Geoffrey looked forward to seeing that book in print. Since he had done so much research he called it "our" book, and hated waiting a year for it to be published.

The year passed and again it was holiday time. We returned to Brixham. The weather was perfect and we had a wonderful time swimming, hiking and picnicking on Dartmoor. We became as brown as chestnuts and felt full of health and vitality.

More than once Geoffrey said, "Do you think our book will be there when we get home?"

It was not, and we were keenly disappointed.

Four days later my husband had a tooth out. I never saw him again. He died under the anaesthetic. On the day of his funeral the postman brought six copies of "our" book. Their arrival added to my grief. Why could they not have come a week earlier?

For days I was too stunned for the full horror of the tragedy to sink in, too shocked for tears. Gradually the nightmare became a reality, and many questions crowded into my mind, demanding an answer: Why had this terrible loss come to *me*? Why should such a fit, strong man die at thirty-nine? How could a God of love allow such a tragedy?

Tearfully, I turned the pages of "our" book and it helped me to find some of the answers. As I read, assurance came that my husband's death had not taken God by surprise. He had allowed it and in the writing of this book He had gently prepared me for what was to come. God knew it would help if I already had my thoughts clarified about death.

But how that book challenged! Did I honestly believe what I had written? With tear-dimmed eyes I read my own words:

> "I remember John telling me of your mother's death, and I was grieved for you," Miss Ormond said. "And yet, you know, we must try not to question God's ways. It's so much easier if we believe that He makes no mistakes, and that these sad things are allowed for a purpose."
>
> "What purpose can there be in someone good getting ill and dying?" Helen asked.
>
> "I once felt just as you do," Miss Ormond replied gently, "but eventually I came to accept Hugh's death as being like a dark thread in the pattern of my life. I couldn't appreciate it, but God gave me the faith to believe that such darkness had been allowed only to show up a particularly beautiful part of His design."

These were the words I had put into my character's mouth. Had I written them with integrity and sincerity?

Geoffrey's death was a thread of deepest black in the pattern of my life. Had God allowed it to reveal a specially lovely part of His design? If He had, my eyes were too tear-dimmed to see it. I clung desperately to the belief that Geoffrey had gone to be with God. One day we would meet again—but desolation engulfed me here and now. Once before I had known desolation like this, briefly and in early childhood.

* * * *

WHEN I was six years of age, my mother took me along the sea front at Westcliff, where we then lived. Usually we walked to the end of the esplanade and back, but this day we kept walking up and down outside a public shelter.

"Why don't we go on, Mummy?" I asked.

"Because we're staying here," she replied.

Then it happened. A strange man came up to her and they talked in low tones, ignoring me completely. Next my mother walked off with the man and left me standing there alone. The sun went behind a dark cloud and I shivered. Tears flowed and I felt utterly desolate.

At last anger came to my rescue. This man was not going to help himself to my mother! I would follow. Where they went I would go too, and off I sped. In fact they went to meet my brother, who broke up from school that day, but they hurried off before he reached the gate.

"Who's that man with Mummy?" Jack asked.

"I don't know but I think it's our father," I whispered with sudden enlightenment. How early feminine intuition develops!

We followed at a distance, still whispering, but I could not stand the suspense.

"I'm going to talk to him," I said, and ran ahead.

I walked unnoticed beside the tall, dark stranger for

some way; then, summoning up all my courage, I spoke to him.

"I'm six," I said.

He must have heard but did not answer. I fell back, rejected, and it did not help when my mother later confirmed that the stranger really was my father.

We lived in a large boarding house but did not eat with the other guests. As we were "permanents" we had our own dining-room where a spotty-faced girl waited on us. She also took Jack and me for walks during school holidays.

"You poor kids!" she said on one walk.

My parents had had a blazing row that lunch-time. They shouted at each other, shouted at us for crying, and yelled at the maid.

When we returned my father had gone. He was home from India on six months' furlough, but spent the rest of it with my grandparents. Furlough came every three years, so I did not see him again until I was nine.

Meanwhile we moved into a flat, quite a novel dwelling-place in those days. My mother believed in keeping herself to herself and I annoyed her by chatting happily to all our neighbours. I also played with some Jewish children who lived in the same block. My mother strongly disapproved and I lost many a Saturday penny through going into their flat. I do not know how many families lived there, but that flat swarmed with children. To me it was great fun the way the babies and toddlers clambered over the furniture in their birthday suits. I wanted to run around naked as well, but was not allowed to. I partly got my own way later by taking off my pyjamas after my mother had said Goodnight.

When the older Jewish children joined the Kindergarten that I attended my mother whisked me off to St. Bernard's Convent. I do not know if this move alarmed my Great Aunt Jane, who was a staunch Anglican, but she suddenly appeared and persuaded my mother to have Jack and me baptised. She had never visited us before and I was fascinated by her huge hat and lethal, spear-like hatpin. She stayed for the baptism and spent a whole day making me a white dress for the service. Some babies were baptised after Jack and I; one yelled lustily. The babies interested me far more than the service.

My mother hoped that I would learn to speak properly and acquire good manners at the convent which was noted for the Perfect Young Ladies it produced. Unfortunately I was one of the failures.

At first St. Bernard's overawed me, not only because of its vast size and the length of its stone-flagged corridors, but also because of the muffled, subdued atmosphere. Nuns moved silently on black plimsolled feet, their heads bowed and hands hidden in the folds of their garments. They never raised their voices, some rarely smiled, and it all puzzled me greatly. Eventually my natural exuberance exerted itself and I was under constant correction. When I ran upstairs, Sister Patrice, the nun who taught me, sent me down again to walk up slowly. When I skipped along a corridor she sent me back to walk demurely, hands at my sides.

Yet I liked Sister Patrice and thought her very pretty. She had lovely smooth skin, pink cheeks and deep blue eyes. Her whole bearing was so holy and serene that sometimes I thought she was a saint.

After morning assembly we girls filed up to our classroom in a long crocodile, Sister Patrice leading the way. She opened our classroom door, then stood to one side as we filed in. A small bowl of holy water hung beside the door and she would nod her approval as we dipped a finger into the bowl and made a sign of the cross on our foreheads.

One day Sister Patrice dropped a folder as she opened the door. All the girls except me walked over it. I stooped and picked it up. Her smile of thanks sent a warm glow right through me.

"How many of you saw this folder on the floor as you came in?" she asked the class, and a sea of hands went up.

"But only one of you had the manners to pick it up," she said. "Stand up, Christine."

Up I stood, proud to bursting point.

But my pride was short-lived. A few days later a nun whom I had not seen before took us for a special session on deportment, manners, and other essentials of a Perfect Young Lady. Oddly enough she did not know we were supposed to leave the room in row after orderly row when lessons ended. I took advantage of her ignorance by dashing out of the room, sliding down the banisters and racing wildly towards the dining-hall. I ran full tilt into a lay sister carrying a pile of dinner plates. The crash of those plates was horrifying and I collapsed into a crumpled heap among the pieces.

For this unruliness I was sent to the Mother Superior whose study lay at the end of a corridor, beyond an archway draped with heavy, plum-coloured curtains. Terrified, I crept through the curtains and knocked timidly at her door. I waited, trembling from head to foot, but nothing happened. I listened at the big keyhole. Silence.

After knocking louder, I heard a soft voice call, "Come in." The Mother Superior looked at me over the top of her steel-framed spectacles and beckoned me to stand by her desk.

"What have you done?" she asked, and now her voice, though still low, had a harsh note.

Vainly I tried to tell her about the plates but my teeth chattered so much that the words got all jumbled up.

"Don't mumble, child," she snapped.

"I . . . I knocked some plates out of a nun's hands, Reverend Mother."

It was out at last and of course she wanted to know the details. After a stern lecture and a bad conduct mark for unruliness she let me go. The conduct mark did not worry me at the time. All I wanted was to escape from that stuffy room and the penetrating gaze of the Mother Superior. It worried me later, though, when Sister Patrice told me that I would be expelled if I gained two more bad marks. Expelled. The word meant nothing to me. But from Sister Patrice's stern look I guessed it must be something dreadful, like being locked up in prison, and it frightened me.

A girl named Doreen sat near me in class and I thoroughly disliked her. She was a smug little Catholic who could recite catechism by the yard. She was also a terrible sneak which trait Sister Patrice encouraged rather than suppressed. Doreen must have disliked me, too, for I was her main target.

"Please, Sister Patrice, Christine's eating toffees again. . . . Christine's copying from Mary's exercise book. . . . Christine's passed Tessa a note. . . ."

Week after week it went on and my dislike turned to bitter hatred. I longed to get even with Doreen Pratt, but fear of another bad conduct mark deterred me.

We had a large cloakroom at the convent, where we hung our clothes on numbered pegs. These pegs were fastened to rows of horizontal poles which were supported at each end by stout, vertical poles from floor to ceiling. Racing up and down the rows was great fun, but forbidden. The horizontal poles were ideal for swinging on but this also was forbidden.

I swung merrily when no one was looking. One day Doreen saw me doing it. She reported me to Sister Patrice and I was in trouble again. Fury burned within me, especially as I had not said anything when Doreen chased her sister up and down the rows of poles.

I had put up with a whole term of Doreen's tale-telling and could stand it no longer. It had got to stop. My chance came when we were alone in the wash-house.

"You beastly sneak!" I fumed, and punched and slapped until her nose and front teeth bled.

She ran screaming from the wash-house and flung herself into Sister Patrice's arms. Between sobs Doreen told her what had happened. The nun's lips set in a hard line but she checked her anger.

"You are a disgrace to the convent," she said icily. "Go home at once. Tomorrow the Mother Superior will deal with you."

I told my brother what I had done and why, and he listened sympathetically.

"You should have bashed her harder and knocked her out, like they do in boxing," he said. "Then she couldn't have split on you."

But I got no such sympathy from the Mother Superior. This time she was expecting me. Her severe look and biting words quickly reduced me to tears of shame and mortification. The worst thing was that I did not want to cry, or feel ashamed. Doreen was a horrid sneak, yet her tale-telling went unpunished. Why should I get all the blame? It was not fair!

"I don't believe you're even sorry," the Mother Superior rasped.

My chin lifted at that. "No, I'm not!" I said.

This confession so maddened her that she grabbed me by the shoulders and shook me. This must have relieved her feelings because she looked at me almost pityingly after that.

"I see no hope for you," she said. "Since you are not a Catholic child the Virgin Mary cannot plead your forgiveness before God. You are sinful and lost. The gate of heaven is closed to you."

All in a flash the answer came. "Oh no! Jesus can unlock the gate and let me in."

The words leaped from eager lips, and the certainty so thrilled me that I must have smiled as I said them. The Mother Superior turned pale with rage. She grabbed me again and shook me until my head swam. Because I added impudence to my other sins she dismissed me with a second bad conduct mark. Only one more and I would be expelled.

It is amazing how I had never lost the simple faith that inspired that "impudent" answer. Four years previously, on Easter Sunday, the proprietor of the boarding-house where we lived invited my mother, brother and me to the Parish Church. The grown-ups all round me sang "There is a Green Hill far away". I wanted to sing too, but being only four, could not read. All the same that hymn touched my heart and brought tears to my eyes.

"Please, Mummy, will you sing me that lovely song, the one about the green hill?" I asked after the service.

My mother could only recall part of the hymn, probably from her Sunday School days, and sang:

> *There was no other good enough*
> *To pay the price of sin;*
> *He only could unlock the gate*
> *Of Heaven, and let us in.*
>
> *He died that we might be forgiven,*
> *He died to make us good. . . .*

Her voice trailed off uncertainly and I was sorry. The wistful tune filled me with exquisite sadness, but the words were beyond me. I asked what they meant and my mother said that Jesus came to die and make people good enough for heaven. She told me what she could, and it was enough. In my simple, childish way I dimly understood that someone called Jesus had died for me and could make me good. It marked the first milestone in my life.

Four years later that tiny, flickering light burst into flame. Its warmth comforted me as I stumbled from the Mother Superior's study and escaped through the plum-coloured curtains.

I learned a lot of catechism and other Roman Catholic teaching at St. Bernard's. But it never obscured that simple, vital belief that Jesus died for me, that He could unlock the gate of heaven and let me in.

Chapter 2

EARLY ESCAPADES

I ENDURED AGONIES of suspense waiting for the term to end and dreaded earning another bad conduct mark. But at least I was clear of Doreen's tale-telling. She was cured—permanently as far as I was concerned! At last we broke up and I was free to shout and jump, free to run and explore and be alone.

One thing marred my happiness. My father was home again on furlough. He filled our tiny flat and had the biggest feet I ever saw. He trod on my toys and it was sickening to see my cowboys and farm animals crushed beneath those huge feet. He swore at me for crying over my broken treasures and generally shouted and bullied. Some days he sat and sulked and my mother nagged him non-stop. Either way I hated him, and hated being indoors.

Most of all I resented my father for spoiling bedtime. Until he came, my mother always read to Jack and me a bedtime story. It was the cosiest thing about our home life. I loved the precious minutes when Jack sat on one arm of her chair and I sat on the other, lost in a world of fantasy.

My father spoilt all that. He had no patience with children's stories and my adventures with Rupert Bear ended. Although we pleaded, mother never read to us again after my father returned to India. Perhaps she thought we were too old for bedtime stories. I know I missed them sorely and only hated my father more bitterly for ending our nightly treat.

But outside life was wonderful—long golden days when the sun shone all day and clouds were non-existent. Neither of my parents worried where I was as long as I did not bother them. I stayed out most of the time, wandering far and wide.

My best friend, Eileen Dawson, was allowed on the beach only when her mother took her. Eileen could not even climb a breakwater without her mother telling her to get down and I pitied her. She knew nothing of the freedom I enjoyed. Sometimes Mrs. Dawson invited me to their safe little picnics but I enjoyed the seashore far more on my own. I roamed happily from Leigh to Southend, making different friends each day. I climbed, paddled, dug dykes and, best of all, played on the warm mud.

Many children like playing in the water but I loved it when the tide was out. The grey mud seemed to spread for miles and I ran and jumped on it to my heart's content. I also rolled in it and let the sun bake it on my skin like a mud pack.

Once I covered Eileen with mud too and her mother was furious. She allowed us no tea until the tide came in and we could wash ourselves clean.

"It doesn't do any harm," I insisted. "I cover myself every day, bathing costume and all. It washes off easily," but Mrs. Dawson remained adamant.

"Grown-ups!" I thought in disgust.

Later I learned that people paid large sums to visit a certain health clinic where they were covered in Westcliff mud. It was reputed to be of great therapeutic value in the relief of rheumatism and other ailments. Well, I got my treatment free.

A creek runs parallel to the shore from Leigh to Westcliff. It is some way out and hidden from the beach. It was a thrill finding that creek. I raced over the warm mud, loving the way it squelched between my toes. Suddenly there was the creek. It wound its shallow way between two high mud banks and I jumped gleefully into it. It never occurred to me, as I splashed happily up and down, what a treacherous enemy that creek could be.

One day I paddled across the creek to the mud flats on the far side. With seagulls as my only companions I ran until I was breathless. I wanted to get to the Thames, which I knew flowed a long way out, but could not reach it.

Suddenly the mud beneath my feet became wet and yielding and the seagulls seemed to screech a warning overhead. I turned and hurried back to the creek. What a change! Gone the shallow, winding water. Gone the high banks. Instead I stared horrified at swirling water rushing upstream. The tide had turned!

I had no idea how deep the creek was, but even in my fright I took no chances. I pulled my dress off before jumping in. My mother had thrashed me recently for having come home wet and bedraggled and I did not want another hiding.

The water reached my chin and I gasped with fright. Holding the dress above my head I waded across the creek. Surging water tugged at my legs. I have a hazy memory of scrabbling with my hands and of the mud giving way under my feet as I tried to climb out. In my terror I lost the dress I had tried to keep dry. The creek claimed it, but miraculously I escaped. My mother never learned what happened to that dress, but I can still see it floating off upstream.

Saturday afternoons held a special treat. Clutching a hot, sticky penny I would run to Leigh-on-Sea, where Nigger Minstrels entertained. They had a little stage on the sand, and never lacked an audience. It cost a penny to sit at the front and I paid up gladly, eager for the fun in store. The minstrels sang and danced and knocked one another about, to the delighted shrieks of their "penny audience". At the end of the show came prize-time when any child who wished could go on the stage and perform a party piece. One girl won a prize every week and I envied her deeply. She could tap-dance and I loved the click of her tap shoes on the bare boards.

One Saturday I learned a poem about a fat and ugly giant. I recited it at the Nigger Minstrel show and, to my delight, won a little box of pink paper and tiny pink envelopes. I treasured that prize greatly and hid it in a safe place where my father could not tread or sit on it.

When I wanted a change from the beach there was always the Underwood to explore. This vast stretch of thicket (now landscaped gardens) covered the hillside near Leigh Station. Local childlore whispered that a mysterious man dressed all in green lived in the Underwood. I spent many hours searching among the hawthorn bushes but never found him.

I knew most of the tracks through the undergrowth but one showery day I lost my way and came to a small clearing where a few gnarled old trees grew. I climbed into one and pure joy filled me as I drank in the scent of the wet, pink blossom. The sun came out while I crouched among the branches and raindrops were transformed before my eyes. They became a myriad diamonds twinkling and sparkling on the leaves. In ecstasy I lingered in that tree. Only when I reluctantly climbed down did I feel the pain of stiff, cramped limbs.

I searched in vain for those gnarled old trees that summer. Never again did I smell that sweet, pink blossom. Yet, even as I write, I sense anew the rapture of that magical glade. A deep love of nature gripped me and God seemed very close that day.

I loved the sunsets, too. On winter Sundays my mother would walk me to the end of the promenade and back, no matter how cold the day or strong the wind. It was never too cold for me to stop and enjoy the sight of the blood-red sun sinking into the sea, tinting the water with its glow. Sometimes little fishing boats would come in with the tide, cleverly following the course of the winding creek. Their sails, red in the sunset, always brought a lump to my throat. Romance and sentiment played a large part in my life.

*　*　*　*

THE long, golden summer ended. My father, still a self-appointed stranger, returned to India and I went back to the convent. A new nun came to us that term, Sister Monique from France. She was very shy, and knew little English, but did her best to teach us needlework. Once she patiently sat beside me trying to teach me French knots. I wanted to please her and she smiled encouragement at my clumsy efforts. At the time I thought she was dumb and felt sorry for her.

Sister Patrice still took us for most subjects and one

morning she told us a harrowing story about African women throwing their babies to the crocodiles.

"The babies are unwanted because they are girls," Sister Patrice went on, "but our missionaries save their lives by buying them from their mothers. If any of you would like to save a black baby, you can buy one for half-a-crown. Bring your money to me this afternoon."

I still had some birthday money left and ran home to take half-a-crown from my money-box. I was anxious to save a black baby from the jaws of a cruel crocodile and was one of the first to give Sister Patrice my rescue money. Several girls gave her half-a-crown and I fidgeted impatiently as Sister Patrice smiled her gratitude.

When she had collected all the money, Sister Patrice told us to open our history books. To my exasperation she then began a lesson. Halfway through the Battle of Waterloo I could stand the suspense no longer and jumped to my feet.

"Please, Sister Patrice, when will the black babies be wheeled in?" I asked.

All eyes turned on me and you could have heard a pin drop.

"What black babies?" Sister Patrice asked icily.

"The ones we've paid for. Can't we choose one this afternoon?" I asked.

A girl tittered and I sensed something was wrong.

"Are you stupid enough to think we have the babies here?" Sister Patrice asked.

She called me to the front of the class as an object of ridicule. She explained that the money was sent to Africa and that the missionaries kept the babies. The other girls tittered and giggled as tears pricked behind my eyes. I was more angry than humiliated.

"Do you mean I can't have the black baby I've paid for?" I asked.

"Of course not! Don't be so silly!" Sister Patrice snapped.

"Then please can I have my half-crown back?"

I had no idea who won the Battle of Waterloo because Sister Patrice sent me out of the room. I sat on the stairs biting my lip and fighting back tears of disappointment. That lunch-time I had eagerly turned out my favourite doll from its pram in cosy readiness for the black baby. I had also robbed it of its vest and rompers and laid them out ready for the little stranger, and carefully washed my toy feeding bottle. The tears flowed. It had all been wasted effort.

Sister Patrice eventually called me back into the class, but she did not return my half-crown. When my disappointment and anger began to die away I became anxious. Would Sister Patrice report me to the Mother Superior for being so stupid? If so, would the Mother Superior give me another bad conduct mark? This time it would mean expulsion.

I worried for days over that bad conduct mark, but the Mother Superior did not send for me and eventually I breathed freely again.

Another memorable history lesson was given by Sister Monique the following term. In halting but moving words she kindled my imagination with her account of Joan of Arc being burnt at the stake "by ze vicked Eenglish". Her face shone with pride as she recounted the courage of this gallant young martyr. I listened spellbound. I, too, wanted to die for a good cause. In years to come people would learn how nobly I had suffered, and would revere my memory.

The only snag was that I did not suffer pain bravely. A few weeks previously I had bruised a toe which turned deep purple and swelled to twice its normal size. Our family doctor gave my mother a kaolin poultice to put on it as hot as could be borne. Every day I cried with the pain. Obviously I was not of the stuff of which martyrs are made. I *had* to teach myself to bear pain. My toe was better by then, but I made myself sit in hotter and hotter baths to get used to the heat of the flames that would one day lick round my stake. In the end I forced myself to sit in such hot water that I scalded both feet and blistered my bottom. It cured me of wanting to be a martyr.

Chapter 3

FRESH FIELDS

WHEN I WAS TWELVE my father returned from India for good. I dreaded his coming, yet it brought some interesting changes. We moved from Westcliff to a brand new house in Surrey. My Great Aunt Jane, who lived at East Sheen, first took my brother and me to see our new home and we were delighted. I loved the smell of fresh plaster and paint and ran excitedly from room to room, my footsteps echoing on the bare boards.

While Jack explored the cupboards under the stairs, I ran through the French doors into the garden. It was a slice of field really with grass waist-high. I knew as soon as I waded into it that I would not miss the Westcliff mud too badly with lovely grass like this to explore and roll in. At the bottom of the garden I caught an enormous green frog. To me it was a thrilling capture but Aunt Jane saw things differently.

"No, you CANNOT take it back to Sheen. No, I do NOT want it in my birdbath," she asserted, and I reluctantly returned the frog to its natural habitat.

We moved a fortnight later and it did not take me long to discover the fields at the bottom of our road. Sheep and cattle grazed contentedly on the lush green grass, a new sight to me. My happiness was complete when I found a friendly old cart-horse drinking his fill from a river meandering through the meadows.

Soon I made friends with two brothers, Trevor and David. They "borrowed" a rope from the nearest building site and tied it to a high branch over the river. We had hours of fun swinging on that rope, and many a ducking when we forgot to lift our feet clear of the water.

Trevor fried sausages and chips on a small fire in our secret den in the bushes. Eager to do my bit, I cooked some apples from an overgrown orchard. The apples were tasty, but the custard was burnt, lumpy and smutty. We ate it all and Trevor generously said my pudding was "very nice". I liked Trevor a lot and any compliment from him was praise indeed.

One day I found four large oil drums stored in our den. Then Trevor and David appeared lugging a length of fencing and two boards that they had "borrowed". The three of us punted happily up and down the river on the raft we made. Providing we spaced ourselves one each end and one in the middle, all went well.

The swallows that flew under a stone bridge fascinated me. I wondered why they liked the bridge so much.

"I reckon they're nesting there," Trevor said, and I urged him to punt under the bridge to see.

"Look! A nest!" David exclaimed, pointing at the overhanging coping.

I jumped forward, eager to see the little mud marvel. The raft dipped sharply shooting us both into the water. It righted itself quickly and Trevor fell in backwards.

If my mother hoped I would keep cleaner now that we had left Westcliff, she was in for a big disappointment. But my brother never got dirty. At Westcliff he spent all his time with his friend Martin, whose father owned a garage. Jack boasted that he helped with repairs but he could not have been much use. He never even got his hands greasy! After we moved he explored Surrey on the bicycle Aunt Jane had bought him, and that kept him clean. Presumably his chain did not fall off as often as mine!

After the summer holiday I went to Hazelwood, a privately owned school run by an elderly lady named Miss Sykes. It took me a long time to settle down there and the other girls made me feel the odd-one-out. When the teacher spoke to me I jumped to my feet. The others tittered at this, but I could not break the habit. It would have been the height of rudeness to answer a nun without standing up.

I sighed with relief the day I left St. Bernard's, but this new school compared badly. Like many things in life, I did not appreciate the convent until I left it.

My disappointment was keen when I saw the Hazelwood gymnasium. It was more like a large barn with a climbing rope hanging from one of the rafters, and little else. My thoughts returned longingly to the convent gym with its parallel bars, vaulting horses, climbing and jumping ropes. The school building was a relic too, with crumbling walls and chimneys that deposited an occasional sooty brick into the fireplace with a triumphant clatter.

Morning assembly was not the formal affair it had been at St. Bernard's but Miss Sykes was simple and sincere. We sang the same hymns with monotonous regularity and I began making friends through my versions of them, which I sang lustily:

Work for the night is coming,
Work till the coming doom,
Fill brightest hours with labour,
Death comes sure and soon.

Some of the girls thought this verse funny and sang it with me. I thought it funny too, for death was a stranger then.

When I moved up into Miss Sykes's class death came closer. A girl called Avril died and Miss Sykes placed a memorial plaque over the fireplace. If she caught us wasting time she would seize the opportunity of delivering her favourite homily. "Minute by minute," she told us, "we should fear the God in whose hand our breath is and not waste the moments He gives. None of us knows how long. . . ." I never listened to any more because her first words carried me into a world of imagination.

I could see God as a venerable, white-haired gentleman holding dozens of coloured balloons by the string. My breath was in one of them. Sometimes I chose a red balloon and sometimes a blue one. Whatever the colour, I hoped that it would not go pop. I also hoped that God would not get angry and squeeze the air out of my balloon. What would become of me if He did? It was a sobering question.

Occasionally a hearse drawn by four black horses would pass our classroom window on its way to the cemetery. Miss Sykes could not see it from where she sat, but I could. At other times a milk cart would clatter by. Either way Miss Sykes took it for granted a funeral had passed and launched into her favourite theme of life's fleeting moments. Sometimes I deliberately banged my desk lid or scraped my feet when horses clopped by—anything to keep Miss Sykes off her pet subject. She dressed, as if she was in perpetual mourning, in a dark grey dress and dark woollen stockings that drooped round her ankles.

Next to funerals, Dickens was Miss Sykes's dearest love. She read us David Copperfield while we industriously plaited raffia mats. I tingled with embarrassment when we hovered by Dora's deathbed while Miss Sykes dabbed her eyes and wiped her spectacles.

One day my friend Wendy accidentally kicked a chunk of plaster from the crumbling wall. Behind wooden slats lay a cavity and beyond that another hole. Wendy and I knelt down to have a closer look and we were mystified. A pair of slippered feet, topped by two ankles clad in striped pyjamas, walked slowly past the hole and back. Wendy and I stared at each other in astonishment.

Who paced that secret chamber? Did Miss Sykes have a prisoner? Was it a man? It must be with big feet and striped pyjamas! We were fascinated and could not rest until we had solved the mystery.

As well as a prisoner, Miss Sykes kept an assortment of animals. She had two dogs, one small and snappy, and the other large and smelly. She also owned numerous cats of various sizes, her favourite being Biddy, the mother of the rest. Then there was a canary in a rusty cage and a seedy looking goldfish in a tiny bowl.

These animals lived in the dingy basement but when a thunderstorm brewed we had the lot in our classroom. Thunder affected the large dog's waterworks, so we all had to lift our satchels off the floor "because poor Twizzle's nervous". The small dog raced madly round the classroom yapping at the cats. As there were a dozen to yap at, concentration on lessons was impossible.

One Monday, Miss Hyatt, my first Hazelwood teacher, took morning assembly. Miss Sykes did not appear. Later it leaked out that, after much suffering, her husband had passed away over the weekend. We were all agog. How could *Miss* Sykes be married? Why had we never seen her husband? Then Wendy remembered the felt slippers and striped pyjamas—the mystery was solved.

After her husband's passing we heard no more from Miss Sykes about "Time's fleeting moments". Perhaps the subject was too painful for her. She became, if anything, even shabbier and thinner. She frequently left the classroom to fetch a glass of hot milk (on doctor's orders, she said) and we were so sorry for her that we never giggled as she sipped it.

Wendy invited me to Crusaders on Sunday afternoons. I had no idea what Crusaders stood for but went because I liked Wendy. It turned out to be a homely Bible Class held in the Assembly Rooms near our school.

I loved Miss Grove, our gentle, kindly teacher, from the first Sunday. She said I would gain a Crusader badge if I came ten Sundays running. I could not wait for those Sundays to pass and it was a proud moment when our Crusader Leader pinned a badge to my blazer.

Miss Grove made the Gospels live for me and it was she who firmly planted Christ in my heart. I *saw* Jesus being baptised in Jordan, saw Him heal the sick, the lame, the blind. As Miss Grove talked, I watched Jesus walk by Galilee, heard Him say to Peter and Andrew "Follow me". I caught glimpses of Him in the Garden of Gethsemane, fought back the tears when they nailed Him to the cross.

Softly and gently Miss Grove revealed the other half of the truth that had been precious since I was four years old. Jesus did die that we might go to heaven. He did die to make us good but, as Miss Grove explained, it is not automatic. We each have to accept for ourselves the salvation and forgiveness that Jesus offers. Although I was too shy to tell her, Miss Grove led me to the feet of the Saviour. He opened my heart and I put my trust in Him.

God's love glowed through Miss Grove, and every girl in her class must have felt its warmth. She told us that God was our Heavenly Father and loved us more deeply than the best human father could do. This was wonderful! It no longer mattered that my father did not love me at all. I had a Heavenly Father Who loved me so dearly that He sent His Son to die for me.

We learned many choruses at Crusaders, including my favourite:

> *Walking with Jesus, by His side I'll stay,*
> *Walking with Jesus in the narrow way;*
> *Travelling along together day by day,*
> *Walking in the King's highway.*

I cannot say when I first thought of my life's journey as walking the King's highway, but I know that I reached the second milestone at Crusaders.

Miss Grove left to be married shortly after my conversion. I missed her sadly, but the little flame of faith she fanned in my heart continued to burn. It may flicker sometimes but it has never gone out.

Chapter 4

THE STORM BREAKS

OUR CRUSADER LEADER, Mrs. Green, often invited us to parties in her lovely garden. We made the most of her swing and see-saw and played games on the lawn. In the winter we had squashes and fireside chats and I enjoyed these even more. They were warm and friendly and Mrs. Green encouraged us in a motherly way to put God first in our lives.

One evening she asked us what we wanted to be when we grew up. I was torn between being a missionary in darkest Africa and a film star in Hollywood, with the scales tipped slightly in favour of the latter. When I told Mrs. Green I wanted to be a film star a deathly silence followed. The girls stared at me, some scornful, some amused and some incredulous. I looked appealingly at our Crusader leader.

"I see, Christine," she said gently, "but maybe God will have something better in store for you. Be sure to walk His way and not your own."

Her earnest words sank in deeply and yet I was puzzled. How could anyone be sure they were walking God's way? I badly wanted to, and cycled home humming my favourite chorus.

*   *   *   *

ILL-HEALTH soon forced Miss Sykes to close her school and I joined my brother at a commercial college.

I went in a state of rebellion because by then I had decided to be a children's nurse and hated the idea of a business training.

Sometimes I cycled across Richmond Park to visit Aunt Jane. She was my godmother and took a keen interest in my future. She sympathised with me and approved of my ambition. She also wrote to several Nursery Training Colleges for me. One prospectus caught my imagination and sympathy. It showed a trainee nursing a black baby. I passionately wanted to do just that, but my parents opposed me. I did not discuss my ambition with my father—we never spoke to each other—but mother told me that he had no time for such crackpot schemes.

"Aunt Jane should mind her own business," my mother snapped. "It's for us to decide what you will do."

For once my parents were in agreement over something! Reluctantly I began a commercial training and hated it.

This college would have come as a shock if Hazelwood School had not partly broken me in. It astonished me to find boys and girls in the same classrooms and I was shocked at the way the older students flirted. Mentally I was still within "convent cloisters". The masters were intimidating, too, especially when they shouted and boxed the boys' ears, which they did quite often.

The master who scared me most was a one-legged Italian named Mr. Neri. No one knew how he had lost his leg, but many wild rumours circulated. Mr. Neri was supposed to teach us Business Routine (or Bus Route as we called it) but he mostly gave us political lectures. He would hoist himself on to a desk, bend his artificial knee with a loud creak, and launch into world affairs. He could see the storm clouds brewing and would berate Neville Chamberlain unmercifully.

"A fat lot of shelter his umbrella will be when the bombs are falling. Pacts! Treaties! Not worth the paper they're printed on! Try holding a bit of paper over your head when your home is falling round your ears! Shout 'Rule Britannia' to deaden the noise!"

He scared the wits out of us and we sat in silent misery. Sometimes he would tell us in lighter vein that soon we would have no need for legs or stomachs. Cars would take us everywhere and we would live on pills. He was ahead of his time, but we thought him a crank. He lived on nuts (which he chewed during lectures) and raw onions, of which he smelt.

He once yelled at me that I may be the apple of my mother's eye—which I certainly was not!—but I would be a pain in the neck to my boss. When I think how little Business Routine he taught, perhaps it was not altogether my fault.

Learning to type was an ordeal, for the teacher as well as for us. We learned touch-typing on machines with blank keyboards and made endless mistakes. Miss Forbes bustled round the class rapping our knuckles for using the wrong fingers. I despaired that my little fingers would ever gain the strength required of them, but they toughened up eventually, to the relief of my knuckles.

To give us a rhythmic touch we typed to music from an old-fashioned gramophone. Even played at its slowest we could not keep up with it, and the distortion was horrible. I still shudder when I think of Rosamunde or William Tell and the way we tortured them to death.

It was from the commercial college that I was sent to my first interview for a job.

"Type this test piece for me," the gentleman said, handing me a printed sheet.

He waved an elegant hand towards a typist's desk and I sat down.

"What an extraordinary typewriter! I've never seen one like this before," I exclaimed.

"And what's wrong with it?" the gentleman asked coldly.

"Well, it's got the alphabet written all over the keyboard!" I said.

He gave me a pained look and did not engage me. I suppose I should have been upset, but my mind was too full of that odd typewriter. I rushed back to college and told the other girls that I had just seen the Eighth Wonder of the World! The headmaster was annoyed that I did not get the job, but I was glad. It meant I could stay on at college a little longer and still see Peter every day. Peter was my boy-friend. We became friends while struggling with book-keeping together. Peter hated the thought of office work as much as I did, but his father had insisted. This made a common bond of sympathy between us which soon ripened into something more tender.

Storm clouds rumbled nearer, daily louder and more threatening. At last, on a September day charged with tension, war was declared. Jack, who had joined the Territorials months earlier, reported to his unit at once, a keen young soldier eager to fight for his country. Fight he did, but three years later he lay down his arms. The battle was over for him, and he was buried in the Military Cemetery in Haifa.

After Jack left home my mother insisted that I should apply for a job at Cable and Wireless, where she had worked before her marriage. My father, who retired shortly before the war in recognition of his foreign service, had already returned to the London office. The young men who had been called up left many vacancies to be filled.

"It's a good firm to work for and you'll get a pension if you don't marry," mother insisted. "Both your grandfathers worked for Cable and Wireless, so you should be proud to carry on the family tradition."

My father strongly opposed this idea, obviously hating the thought of having me around his office as well as his home. Since one office was as bad as another to me, my mother won the day and I applied. My father did not know that I went for an interview. He was furious when I began work at Electra House. Fortunately it is a large building and we seldom met in the entrance or corridors. If ever our timing was bad, he would look the other way and not see me.

Aileen, Jean and Marie began work on the same day as I did and we made a friendly foursome. At first we found plenty to giggle about, but sobered up when the London air raids began. Travelling became a nightmare. A half-hour journey could take three hours or more when the railway received a direct hit. Once or twice I was tempted to break our silence barrier and plead with my father to take me home. He knew all the alternative routes, whereas I knew none, but I could never quite bring myself to ask him.

Above all else, I hated travelling by Underground. It was heartbreaking to see elderly, war-weary folk lugging their mattresses down to the comparative safety of the Tube for the night. It was even worse stepping over those who had already staked their pitch on the platform, and to smell the sweat and stale urine.

When sleeping accommodation became available in the basement of Electra House I welcomed it gladly. I and my three friends applied for bunks at once. To our delight we shared a small store room. The heat nearly stifled us, but that was nothing compared with the discomforts of travelling every day.

The canteen where we spent our evenings offered no better ventilation. Here the smell of beer and tobacco added to the fug. It caused no problem to the R.A.F. trainees responsible. They had come to Electra House to learn telegraphy and crowded eagerly into the canteen when the day's training ended.

We often chatted to the trainees but some of them treated us like schoolgirls and I disliked the way they teased us. Marie developed an outsize crush on one of them and spent every spare minute knitting gloves and socks in Air Force blue. Her heart-throb never wore them because his draft was whisked away. A new draft replaced it and the fug in the canteen continued.

By the autumn we were sick of the canteen with its beer and smoke. One evening we pottered about in our basement bedroom trying to tidy up but only getting in each other's way.

"Phew! Let's go out!" Jean exclaimed.

"Curfew's at eight and it's quarter to now," ·Marie objected.

"Long enough for a breath of air," Aileen said, and off they went.

I shoved my clothes back into a case and ran after them.

"Where d'you think you're going?" the sentry demanded, barring the door with his rifle.

"Only along the Embankment."

"O.K., but don't be long," he grunted.

"What lovely cool air! Let's go up on the bridge," Jean
said. "We can walk on the other side of the river to
Blackfriars."

We had no idea how far it was. The air-raid warning
sounded as we crossed Waterloo Bridge. Should we go
on? We decided to risk it but were soon dismayed at the
distance to Blackfriars.

"Blow these slippers!" I exclaimed.

I had come out in a hurry wearing tatty old slippers
and could not keep up with the others without their
falling off.

Blackfriars at last! Suddenly anti-aircraft guns
opened fire and shrapnel hit the bridge as we crossed
it. Then a violent explosion rocked the buildings
in New Bridge Street. In terror, we took to our
heels.

I limped into Electra House after the others, having
run barefoot along the Embankment. We were
exhausted and gasping for breath, but the sentry
showed no sympathy.

"You darned fools, you do ask for it!" he shouted.
"No, you can't go to the canteen. Stay here until the
Sergeant comes."

We sat anxiously in the guard-room. Would we be
sacked? We knew that could mean a munitions factory
for us, and did not fancy it.

The Sergeant came at last, grey-haired and tired-
looking.

"Look, girls, be sensible and stay indoors," he said in

fatherly tones, and that was that. It was quite an anticlimax really.

We heard no more bombs that night, but felt the ground shake as we lay in our bunks. Our basement bedroom seemed secure and we felt safe.

Then the flying bombs came, sinister in flight and devilish in their destruction. Relief was great when one passed overhead with the engine still running. Once it cut out you were lucky if you had time to reach safety. One weekend a flying bomb hit the side of Electra House and exploded on the second floor. Great chunks of masonry crashed through the pavement into the basement where we slept on weeknights and a voluntary nurse was killed. So much for our safe shelter! None of us had realised that the pavement was the roof to that part of the basement. Thank God it happened at the weekend or the casualties would have been far greater.

Huge tanks on the fifth floor burst when the bomb struck and tons of water cascaded down the staircases, filling the lift shafts and flooding the basement. Ceilings collapsed, windows shattered and doors fell crazily across corridors. Grit, plaster and water combined to make a thick paste underfoot.

Chaos greeted me that Monday. A heap of masonry sprawled over the road and glassless windows gaped hideously. I entered the building and climbed the gritty stairs. No one saw me as the Home Guards and wardens were busy clearing the basement. I clambered over doors and rubble until I reached my office. Both walls had fallen to form an arch. I could see my typewriter and crawled in to rescue it, only to find it choked with rubble and useless.

The office my boss used had almost disappeared. The

furniture had fallen through a gaping hole in the floor, where his carpet flapped sadly in the wind.

Among the debris I found a fat query file. I hated that file! It contained papers I had no idea what to do with. The problem solved itself that day—I threw the file through the hole. Just in time too. A warden caught me crawling about and sent me home.

The night telegraphists showed great courage when that bomb struck. While wardens kept watch on the roof, they calmly sent messages all over the world. Suddenly a warden yelled over the inter-com, "This is it! Duck for your lives!"

Transmission stopped for twenty minutes until light and power were restored. Operators crawled from their hiding places and returned to work. Amid clouds of dust and rubble they continued transmitting and no one overseas guessed that we had been bombed.

As a communications centre Electra House was a main target, so strict secrecy was enforced. After the war, when the staff magazine released details of the damage, letters arrived from far and wide expressing sympathy and surprise. Expressions of admiration came also for the night operators who bravely carried on working without betraying what had happened.

I could not be numbered among the brave. That bomb proved so unnerving that I never slept in Electra House again.

Chapter 5

THE THIN END OF THE WEDGE

MY PRAYERS DURING THE WAR could hardly be called deep communion with God. Mostly I asked for His protection during air raids, but often forgot to thank Him for my safety. In my heart I knew this was not enough and often thirsted for something warmer, closer.

Although I got on well with Aileen, Jean and Marie, they often irritated me by chatter that never went much beyond eligible airmen, hair curlers, and how to make do until the next clothing coupon ration. My need for spiritual fellowship led me to pray for a Christian friend. There must be at least *one* other Christian girl in the building. If only our paths could cross!

This became a daily burden and I looked impatiently for an answer. One day I took some papers down to the Company Secretary's department. The girl who took them from me stared at my Crusader badge while I gaped at her Covenanter badge and the papers were forgotten. We smiled at each other and became instant friends. God's answer had come and this time I remembered to thank Him.

Joan told me that she, too, had prayed for Christian friends and longed for a prayer fellowship in Electra House.

"With over 2,500 people working here we can't be the only Christians," Joan asserted.

"Probably not, but how do we find the others?" I asked.

"How did we find each other? We'll pray about it," Joan answered brightly. "Let's ask God to show us if He wants us to form a Christian fellowship. If we find eight more Christians we'll take that as His seal."

I thought this was asking a lot of God, especially as Joan expected a quick answer. It amazed me to watch His answer unfold. First Joan met Dorothy, another Crusader, in the canteen. Dorothy knew of two more girls who would be interested in a prayer meeting. They worked together on the sixth floor. Next a young fellow followed me into the lift. I stared unbelievingly at his Scripture Union badge. He knew another Christian chap. I then found that our permanent auditor was a Christian. . . . So it went on until, like the little nigger boys, we numbered ten.

Joan immediately asked the Company Secretary if we could have a room to meet in weekly for Christian fellowship. Space was scarce but the Secretary was sympathetic and allocated us a storeroom in the basement, the best available. There we sat on wooden benches surrounded by dusty files.

But when our Chairman, Sir Edward Wilshaw, heard about us, he had different ideas. He decided to build us a chapel!

I could hardly believe it when Joan told me. We would all appreciate a more inspiring room than that scruffy store—but a chapel! Joan's eyes shone with excitement and pleasure.

In spite of the war and scarcity of materials, plans

went ahead. Soon the lovely little chapel was ready. I gazed in awe at windows hung with royal blue velvet curtains and at the rich carpeting of the same shade. On either side of the blue and gold altar hung a memorial tablet bearing the names of staff who had died in both world wars. Sir Edward had even provided us with several Bibles beautifully bound in real leather.

His generosity and interest touched me deeply, yet I disliked the publicity that the chapel brought to Joan and me. Suddenly we were in the news and I was sent for to be photographed in the chapel. It gave me no pleasure to see my picture in the papers the next day.

The Archbishop of Canterbury, Doctor Lang, dedicated the chapel and said that it was unique—he knew of no other chapel within a great London business house. He thought it most moving that in such a building, with its ceaseless activity, there should be such a place of peace.

The service was relayed throughout the building and many of the staff had a share in it. Sir Edward Wilshaw and other directors were in the chapel itself with members of the staff picked by ballot. Neither Joan nor I were picked, and I was relieved. It was all too overwhelming for me.

I listened with mixed feelings to the service and looked wonderingly at the staff who packed the staircase leading to the chapel. Many had openly criticised its being built and scorned the Christian Union. All at once religion had become popular and here they were enjoying the pomp and ceremony of the Messengers' Band playing in the entrance hall to Electra House.

How far removed all this was from the simple devotional meetings that meant so much to our little fellowship. None of us wanted all this publicity and show, least of all Joan and I. My misgivings were greater than Joan's. This was partly because my thinking had already become coloured by the teaching of Clive, a new friend of only a few weeks' standing.

I had been struggling to overcome a bout of depression when I first met Clive. In addition to the war outside, my parents were going through alternate phases of violent quarrelling and long sulks. The sulky patches were the hardest to bear. We sat for whole evenings in silence. Relief from the tensions of my parents' private war only came with the wailing of the air-raid siren. It forced my attention on wider horizons.

I never screamed during an air raid but often came near to it over the private battle within our four walls. How could I escape from it? I no longer slept at Electra House and it was dangerous to go out after dark. I longed for another Christian friend, one who lived close by whom I could visit in the evenings with comparative safety. Yet it seemed greedy to ask God for another friend when Joan meant so much to me. If only my boy-friend Peter could be around more often, but he was away building landing barges in some secret boat yard.

One Friday I left the office with a heavy heart. My parents had not spoken to each other for a week and I dreaded the sight of their set, sphinx-like faces. I got out of the train at Motspur Park and slowly walked the long road home. Dusk fell and yet there was enough light for a passing cyclist to spot my Crusader badge. He braked and called out to me, which was embarrassing as I had to wipe the tears away before facing him.

With a friendly grin he introduced himself as Alf.

"I assume from your badge that you're a Christian," he said, and I managed a smile as I nodded.

We chatted a long time and Alf was surprised when I told him where I lived. He could not understand why I left the train at Motspur Park when I lived at Tolworth, and I did not enlighten him.

Alf told me about his friend Clive, who also lived at Tolworth, and knew the Bible from cover to cover. It turned out that Clive lived in the next road to me. Alf invited me to the Bible studies held in Clive's house. At first I refused but he persisted and offered to call for me if I felt shy. I did not want him to call. No one ever called at our house! But I eventually agreed to meet Clive and his wife Lillian.

Lillian was only eighteen. They had not long been married. As a stranger to the district she welcomed my friendship as much as I did hers. With Clive I was not so at ease. He had an autocratic bearing which created respect rather than friendship.

Four young men who worked in the same firm as Clive came to the Bible studies. Like mine, theirs was a reserved occupation, which meant they could not be called up for military service. I told them about the chapel being built in Electra House and they showed great interest, except for Clive. He remained oddly quiet.

I had an insatiable thirst for Bible knowledge and thought Clive a wonderful teacher. We spent many happy hours poring over the Scriptures together.

"How long have you been a Christian?" Clive asked one evening.

"Since I was twelve but I've only been a dormant one most of the time," I confessed, flushing uncomfortably.

He nodded gravely and exhorted me to go on in the Christian faith and learn more of God's Word.

"I want to," I assured him, "but up to now I've had no one to teach me. You see I was converted at Crusaders but when war started we lost our hall and most of the teachers left. Now we meet in the leader's house, but she has to teach us all together. The youngest girls are only ten, so we older ones don't learn much."

Again Clive nodded gravely. "What about church connections?" he asked.

"Well, I was confirmed when I was in the Guides but it didn't mean much. My friend had hiccoughs most of the service and I had the giggles."

"I see."

"I didn't like the vicar anyway," I went on. "He asked to see me before the confirmation service. When I told him of my Crusader connections he didn't approve. He maintained that Crusaders kept young people from corporate worship in the church. I explained that I was converted to Christ at Crusaders but he didn't seem to understand. As I didn't know what he meant by corporate worship either, I never went to church after my first communion."

Little did I realise that I was leaving myself wide open to attack!

"Sardis! Sardis!" Clive muttered.

This puzzled me until I discovered that the Exclusive Brethren, with whom Clive was associated, referred to the Church of England as the Sardis of Revelation 3.

They regard themselves as Philadelphia, the church "with a little strength" and the one in which Christ finds nothing to condemn.

Gradually Clive's teaching became more "slanted". He told me that anything to do with "worldly systems of religion" was wrong, even Satanic. He expressed horror when I told him that the chapel had been dedicated by the Archbishop. He said bluntly that if I wanted to walk in the light which Christ gave to His faithful followers, I would have to separate from all forms of "unsound" organised religion. He asserted that the truth could be found only outside such systems.

I wanted the truth more than anything else but was astonished and bewildered by Clive's statement that Christianity as practised by the Established Church was entirely unscriptural. Fancy such a huge organisation being so utterly misguided!

While I thought about this I still lapped up the Christian doctrine Clive taught and, like Oliver Twist, continually wanted more. My imagination took wings as we studied Ephesians together. Not for me the noble martyrdom of convent days. Now I would LIVE for God and do great things for Him. I wanted the whole armour of God, and to know all truth. My feet would carry the gospel of peace as I strode forth with the shield of faith and helmet of salvation. With the sword of the Spirit for my weapon I would dare anything for God.

So much for my imagination, but things did not work out that way. God had yet to teach me that a spoonful of experience gained while walking life's path with Him is worth more than a bucketful of head knowledge. But experience is often painfully acquired.

"Why do you wear that Crusader badge?" Clive asked me on one occasion.

"To show that I'm a Christian," I replied.

"It's a poor sort of Christian who needs a badge to show it," he said.

A well aimed dart this, and it hit home. From that moment I seriously questioned my ways. Where was I going? Who with? Why? Was it the right path anyway?

Chapter 6

BY-PATH MEADOW

I F EVER I WAS RESTLESS, it was then. Rebellious too, yet still wanting God's truth. How could it be wrong to wear a Crusader badge? Crusaders had guided my feet towards the King's highway. I looked up to the leader as a fine Christian woman. Was she really guilty of some unscriptural error? Then again, God had used my badge. Through it I met Joan and Alf. Would God use a wrong thing?

I still went to Clive's Bible studies but remained confused and silent until he asked me outright what was wrong.

"It's what you said about my Crusader badge," I blurted out. "I wouldn't even be here if it wasn't for that."

Clive smiled, explaining that God bears with us in our weaknesses and goes on with us where we are.

"But He doesn't expect us to remain babes in Christ, wanting toys and rattles for ever. He expects us to grow up and equip ourselves with His armour, not with badges." Clive's face became stern, almost severe. "If you are really sincere, God will lead you on to a higher walk and greater truth, but first you'll have to give up 'badge Christianity', squashes, fireside chats and the rest of it."

I listened in troubled silence.

"Don't forget Christ was rejected by the religious leaders of His day," Clive went on. "Why should you expect anything different? Who are *you* to command more favourable recognition than your Saviour?"

Clive's words presented a challenge, demanded a decision. Still I hung back, weighing the pros and cons, counting the cost. We talked until late and Lillian invited me back to tea the next day, a Saturday. I explained that I could not come because I was meeting Peter, my boy-friend. Inwardly I was glad of a legitimate excuse. It would give me time to get my wind back after the spiritual battering that Clive had given me.

When next I saw Clive he asked me about Peter and I told him that we had been friends since our college days.

"Is he a Christian?" Clive asked.

"No, which is a pity because he knows the Gospel message as well as I do. He treats salvation as a joke, saying that's something to worry about when you're old," I said.

"Why don't you give him up?"

Clive's question shocked me and I explained that I prayed regularly for Peter and hoped to win him for the Lord. Also, since we were very fond of each other, we intended to marry after the war.

Clive shook his head and told me that marriage to a non-believer would mean an unequal yoke. He read me the verse in Deuteronomy which says that an ox and an ass should not be yoked together.

"The two would not pull evenly, you see," Clive explained, "and neither will you and your boy-friend if you marry. While you hunger for the Lord's green pastures, your yoke-fellow will drag you off to feed on thistles."

It was all very upsetting. I wanted to do such great things for God and come through spiritual warfare with flying colours. Instead, through Clive, I believed He was simply asking me to give up Peter. Nothing spectacular there, hardly anyone would know about it. Only Peter and I would suffer. It was not fair!

That night I lay awake re-living the tender moment in the college cycle shed when Peter first kissed me. I wept when I remembered the blotting paper we swallowed with a heart and each other's name on it. We had thought so much of each other ever since. Was it all to end now?

And what of the Crusaders? I loved our leader and was reluctant to leave her, though I was really too old for her class. How could I hurt her by telling her I "had seen the light" and could no longer wear a Crusader badge?

Harder still, what about Joan and our meetings? Would God truly not take me on in the Christian life until I separated from this small segment of a "worldly religious system"?

After days of misery and inward struggle I told Clive defiantly that I intended giving up nothing.

"I am not asking you to," he replied coldly. "I have only shown you the principles the Lord has set out in His Word. You have a free choice of action, but I can tell you this. The Lord will lead you no farther along His highway until you obey Him where you are. You may be halted for years at this very milestone. As I've said before, it's only when we surrender in obedience to

Him that the Lord leads us to a higher path of communion with Himself."

These words could justifiably have been spoken by any Christian leader but in this instance a misguided man used them in seeking to draw me from the true highway into a by-path that he sincerely believed to be the right way.

The inner battle continued to rage. So all absorbing did it become that I did not even notice when my parents were on speaking terms and when they were not. Part of me pulled one way, part the other, and my distress was great.

Victory, if it could be called that, came in stages. First I left Crusaders and the leader bade me a sad, fond farewell.

"Do nothing in haste," she counselled. "Be very sure." But her wisdom fell on deaf ears.

Next I broke with Peter. That hurt far more, and I doubted if I would marry after that.

"Not that it matters. I've never seen much to recommend marriage," I consoled myself.

For further consolation I revived earlier girlhood dreams of the little flat I would one day rent, where I would live alone and in peace.

Last of all came Joan, the dear friend whom I admired in so many ways. It would look so disloyal to leave her. Would she understand? And what would the others think who met with us in the chapel at Electra House? Worst of all, how would I bear the loss of Joan's friendship as well as Peter's?

After the distressing parting with Peter, I recoiled from telling Joan face to face of my eventual decision. Instead I took the coward's way out and wrote her a letter before going on holiday. In it I told her I would not be coming to the chapel any more, explaining why as best I could. In spite of her sorrow, she sent me a sweet and gracious reply, but said she was positive I had made a big mistake.

After these apparent victories, it was with a sense of triumph that I told Clive of my severed worldly connections. What did I expect next? Some special shower of heavenly blessing perhaps. Certainly I looked for congratulation from Clive, but there was none. I was totally unprepared for what happened.

Clive, in an oddly detached manner, told me that he had taken me as far as he could spiritually. He said I needed deeper fellowship with more mature Christians. It sounded crazy! How could anyone be more mature than Clive? He assured me there were many such people and produced the addresses of three suitable meeting places: the Open Brethren, the Kelly Brethren and the Exclusive Brethren. He said that all three were free from the errors of traditional church systems, but added: "Don't go to the last address until you've tried the others."

I felt like a fledgling pushed from its nest. Those precious Bible studies had ended and Clive pointed the way to some new horizon. Alf and the others turned their backs on this new horizon. It was too demanding on their personal lives and loyalties. But I now had no strong ties and was prepared to go to all lengths to find more Truth.

I looked at the three addresses and wondered what was odd about the Exclusive Brethren. I decided to visit them first instead of last. And so, to borrow a name from *Pilgrim's Progress,* I walked all unsuspecting through the gate into By-path Meadow, a gate that was to shut firmly behind me.

The following Sunday I went in search of the nearest Exclusive Assembly. The hall, built of dull yellow bricks, was set back from the road. I would have passed it by but for the small notice nailed to the wall. It read "The Word of God is preached here every Sunday evening at 6.30." (Today you would find no such landmark. The Exclusive Brethren no longer advertise their gospel meetings in this way, since outsiders are not encouraged to attend.)

Timidly, I then entered the hall. Most of the Brethren were already assembled, since it was almost time to celebrate the Lord's Supper, as the Communion Service is called. Another notice confronted me with the words, "Will those known in fellowship and the breaking of bread please sit in front of this board." I sat behind it and gazed in awe at the rows of bowed heads.

In the centre of the hall stood the Lord's Table covered in a white cloth. On it were a loaf of bread, a cup of wine and a collection basket. The brothers and sisters sat in four blocks of chairs, all facing the table, with leading brothers in the front rows.

How dull the sisters looked in their drab coats and hats pulled down over their foreheads! No one dressed all that smartly during the war, but somehow these sisters looked extra dowdy. This I put down to their "other worldliness".

The meeting began with a hymn chosen from a book of Spiritual Songs for the Little Flock. We sang slowly and dolefully, unaccompanied by instruments of any kind. Clive had told me that brothers would announce hymns, pray or "minister from the Word" as led by the

Holy Spirit and I expected spiritual power to surge through me like an electric shock, too. To my disappointment nothing like that happened. The meeting was slow and undramatic, with long periods of silence between each hymn and prayer. Some brothers looked as if they were in a trance, others lost in meditation. Even the small children sat motionless gazing into space.

The afternoon Bible Reading impressed me far more and I listened spellbound to a brother expounding the Epistle to the Romans.

No one spoke to me that day, but the following Sunday the leading brother, Mr. Barnes, asked me my name and whether or not I was a believer. He was a small man with piercing eyes and a thin nose with a drip on the end of it. The drip wobbled when he spoke and it worried me a lot. I did not like the idea of it falling on the Bible he clasped with both hands.

When Mr. Barnes had satisfied himself that I was a seeker after the truth he invited me to tea. Mrs. Barnes, a large woman with a subdued but gracious manner, led me to her bedroom to leave my coat and the hat I had bought specially for Brethren meetings. As I turned to leave the room Mrs. Barnes indicated a commode and suggested I might like to use it. She explained that it would be indiscreet to go to the toilet since several brothers had come for tea and they would be using it. I declined politely and made a mental note to drink only one cup of tea.

The most gratifying impression of that tea-party was that the brothers appeared greatly surprised by my knowledge of Scripture. They questioned me closely as to where I had gained such knowledge and I told them about Clive's Bible Study group. Unknown to me they began immediate enquiries and it eventually transpired that Clive had been a member of the Exclusive Brethren in another part of the country but had recently left them over some doctrinal quarrel. His teaching still bore a strong Exclusive slant which Mr. Barnes was quick to detect from my replies to his questions.

The Brethren taught me still more doctrine in the weeks that followed and I enjoyed a good deal of hospitality. I also made friends with several young brothers and sisters, and discovered that the main objective of the latter was to get an Exclusive husband as soon as possible. At the time it struck me as a very "fleshly" ambition!

Clive still invited me to his home and questioned me as closely about the Brethren as they did about him. He also told me his version of why he had left the Exclusives but doctrinally it was quite beyond me.

I hated sitting alone behind that wretched board and eventually, with fear and trembling, asked for fellowship. Some of the younger sisters had already warned me that I would be asked some "terribly hard" questions before being accepted, but in fact I was asked very little. Apparently I had already given all the right answers in general conversation. The Brethren merely wanted to satisfy themselves that I had no "worldly links". I assured them that I had broken with all those months before. No, I never went to the cinema or theatre, and Mr. Barnes nodded his approval. I did not tell him this was because I was saving hard to furnish a flat, rather than from any conviction regarding the sinfulness of such places, as I knew this would weigh against me.

After my case had been discussed at a Care Meeting, which I was not eligible to attend, I was recommended for fellowship and received the news by letter. It pleased me enormously that the Brethren considered me suitably unworldly. My heart beat fast when I took my place in front of the board the following Sunday. It missed a beat or two, though, when Mr. Barnes suddenly jumped to his feet and hurried towards me, the drip on his nose wobbling anxiously.

"A last minute snag," I thought in dismay.

"Have you been baptised?" Mr. Barnes asked, the drip dangerously near my ear.

"No, but I was christened when I was seven," I whispered.

"That's all right, as long as you've had the name of Christ called over you," he said, much relieved.

Some weeks later, Ruth, the eldest daughter of one of the Brethren, asked for fellowship. Before she could be received she had to be baptised. This "ceremony" took place in a leading brother's bathroom. Ruth appeared in a thick, white nightdress with long sleeves, which she borrowed from Mrs. Barnes. She tucked her lovely hair under a bathing hat on top of which she wore an ordinary hat. Mr. Barnes baptised her in the bath. The hat was removed for this operation, but returned to her head immediately afterwards. She looked so ridiculous kneeling on the floor in a pool of water while prayers were offered that I was heartily thankful to Great Aunt Jane for seeing to my christening.

Once I was in fellowship I repeatedly asked Clive and Lillian to come to the meetings.

"Whatever you had against the other meeting you went to, I'm sure you'll be happy with these Brethren," I assured Clive, and was delighted when eventually he and his wife came along.

When they too asked for fellowship my joy knew no bounds. My only worry in those early days was the drip on the end of Mr. Barnes's nose! It wobbled precariously when he drank from the Communion cup, which would soon be passed to me. It never actually dropped in, but it gave me many anxious moments.

When I joined the Exclusive Brethren I was convinced that they were the only Christians who were "right". My limited experience of ministers had been singularly unimpressive as they lacked authority. The Brethren, by contrast, spoke so confidently of doctrine, prophecy and interpretation of the Bible that I could hardly be blamed for believing that I had found an oasis in a spiritual desert.

At the close of a weeknight Bible Study, I overheard an elderly sister say, "We spend so much time learning Christian theory that there's none left to practise it." If ever I heard the truth without recognising it, it was then. Her remark so shocked me that I turned round and glared at her. My thirst was still so great for doctrine that I failed to see the need for practical Christianity.

Contact with neighbours or friendships outside the Assembly were frowned upon because we had to be "separate" to be used by Christ. Somehow it never occurred to me to wonder how I could witness to those around me if I never spoke to them. As to helping anyone in need, how could we when we would not even have known about it?

So there I was in By-path Meadow, a meadow hedged high with numerous rules, mainly "Thou shalt nots". I accepted these taboos cheerfully, since it was worth any sacrifice to gain the Truth. The Brethren certainly knew their Bibles and I marvelled at their interpretation of obscure verses. How slowly it dawned on me that knowledge, like faith, is dead without works!

I was not discerning enough to realise that many Bible verses were torn from their context and the "meaning" stretched to a point that bore little relation to the original meaning. But, in all fairness, this fault is not confined to the Exclusive Brethren.

Typical of this distortion was the story of the Good Samaritan. A man travelling down from Jerusalem to Jericho (the wicked world) is left half dead by thieves. A priest (representing organised religion) passes by without helping. Next a Levite (the Mosaic Law) has a look and passes on. Then a Samaritan (a "religious" outcast) comes UP the road and helps the stranger.

The Brethren maintained they were best fitted to help the spiritually wounded because they were going UP towards the heavenly Jerusalem. All others go DOWN the road.

This interpretation was one of the first things to raise doubts with me. The Bible says nothing about the Samaritan going in the opposite direction. From where, I wondered, did the Brethren glean this piece of information? Again, it would be most unlikely that a despised Samaritan would go to Jerusalem anyway.

At last I began to think for myself and not absorb everything without question. But it disturbed me. If the Brethren were wrong, then where could the truth be found?

I was further disturbed when Mrs. Barnes's domestic help told me of an incident in that house. Mr. Barnes had invited several Brethren to dinner without giving his wife much warning. Although the Brethren regularly received generous food parcels from "the saints" abroad during the war, catering for a dozen extra still presented a problem.

That morning Mr. Barnes took ages reading his mail at breakfast. His wife, normally meek and subdued, asked him to hurry up. Without replying, Mr. Barnes opened his Bible and read her Leviticus until eleven o'clock as a lesson in subjection! Her daily help found her in the kitchen in tears of frustration. This infuriated me. In her place I would have walked out of the house and left Mr. Barnes to cater for his own guests, and said so to the daily help.

"But dearie, 'er 'usband's the 'ead of the 'ouse, what can she do?" she wailed.

"*Walk out!*" I repeated.

After that Mr. Barnes's teaching carried little weight with me. A man devoid of love and consideration for his wife was not worth listening to. I recalled the elderly sister's remark: "We spend so much time learning about Christianity that there's none left to practise it." Could she be right after all? The suggestion alarmed me but I banished it from my mind.

Why did I not leave the Brethren at this point? I have been asked that question several times. All I can say is that fetters of fear already bound my feet. The Brethren had brainwashed me into believing that it was a terrible sin to turn one's back on the truth as found in the Assembly. They talked darkly of the judgment of God that would surely follow and I was terrified of incurring His wrath. Fear paralyzed me into doing nothing but make excuses.

Failure of some of the Brethren to live up to Christian

standards there might be, but who was I to condemn? Occasional biblical distortion there certainly was, but then my own understanding of the scriptures was far from perfect, so was this a valid reason for walking out?

As a seeker after the Truth I desperately wanted to believe that the Brethren, as a body, really were the custodians of that Truth. I had given up so much to find it, separating myself from my dearest friends for the Truth's sake. If the Brethren did not possess it, where else could I hope to find it? Despair engulfed me. More than anything else, I dreaded being lost in a spiritual No Man's Land where an angry God would abandon me.

Chapter 7

HOME SWEET HOME

NO MORE FLYING BOMBS, no more rockets or wailing sirens. The war ended at last, and victory was celebrated with a national holiday.

We younger Brethren went off for a day in the country. We swam, picnicked and basked in the sunshine. The older brothers frowned on this "unseemly exploit" and told us we should have spent the day more profitably by studying our Bibles. Once I might well have agreed, but now my attitude was changing. With the grim war years over I wanted gaiety and fun. I still look back on that golden, gloriously free day as one of the happiest of my life.

I came in for extra rebuke because I did not wear a hat on this spree. Nowadays sisters cover their heads with a scarf but then a hat was regarded as essential, being a "token of subjection" to men. Brothers, too, wore hats to acknowledge the headship of Christ. Also, as one brother said to me, how could a man uncover his head to pray (as instructed in 1 Corinthians 11) if he did not wear a hat to start with? I was never quite clear on the "hat doctrine" but gathered it was also something to do with the angels looking on—angels being referred to in the same chapter. The Exclusive Brethren took the whole matter very seriously, and one hoary-headed old brother would not go into his garden without wearing a straw hat with a narrow brim and crown like a huge pudding basin. I often wondered if that hat amused the angels as much as it did me.

I often went without a hat, as most girls did. At least, I prided myself, I have long hair. On the day we went swimming it surprised me to find that the sisters with me had only shoulder-length hair. Since they usually wore it in a roll it was impossible to tell its length. But these girls were born and bred in Brethren households and their fathers taught in the meetings that it was shameful for a woman to cut her hair. Obviously they did not know what went on in their own homes.

Although the war had ended, there was no peace treaty in my home. I was weary with the rows and began looking for a small unfurnished flat. I might just as well have wanted an apartment on the moon; but I never gave up hoping and looking.

Often I lay awake at night mentally furnishing my own little home. The colour scheme never varied. I would have a beige carpet patterned with orange and green, and a settee and two armchairs in the same shade of green. The curtains would be basically oatmeal, boldly patterned in green, brown, orange and yellow. My table, chairs and bedroom furniture would all be in a medium shade of oak.

This dream began as a schoolgirl, and when I left school I had thirty pounds saved up in the Post Office towards the cost of furniture. I lived frugally during the war, never spending money on the cinema, make-up or hair-do's. Every penny was tucked away for the flat. My clothes, too, were bought to last, though I was hardly alone in this. With clothing strictly rationed and the accent on utility, I dressed very much according to the fashion of the time.

When the war ended I had saved enough to furnish a small flat, and was wildly excited when I was offered an ideal one in Raynes Park. It seemed too good to be true and I wondered if there could be a snag. I soon found out. That flat would be mine only on payment of five hundred pounds "key money", which was more than my savings. Had I possessed the money I would have been unhappy at obtaining the flat by bribery.

The search continued for several years. My health suffered under the continual frustration and I became very nervy. It became increasingly hard to go home when my day's work was done and I would trudge up the road on unwilling feet.

"Surely God doesn't want me to live like this much longer!" I exclaimed to Lillian one day, and she encouraged me to go on believing that God had a plan for my life, which He would reveal step by step.

"But I've been walking on this dreary stretch of road for so long," I complained.

It did not help when Lillian pointed out that many demobbed soldiers and their wives still had no homes of their own, but lived in overcrowded conditions with unwilling parents.

Then the Brethren put pressure upon me. They insisted that, since I was of age, it was not right that I should continue to live with non-Christian parents.

"You should rent accommodation where you can entertain your brothers and sisters in Christ, and be separate from worldly influences," they said.

"There's nothing I'd like better. Perhaps the Brethren will help me find a flat," I suggested eagerly.

They cooled off at that and not one of them offered so much as a bed-sitter in their own spacious homes. Their lack of response was disappointing and I was acutely conscious of their lack of love and genuine concern.

Mr. Edgar, for whom I worked at the time, showed far more interest. He knew something of my background because my father's behaviour during the war had angered him. He had often seen him hurrying off after work, leaving me to find my own way home in all the travel problems.

"I don't wonder you're nervy living with that lot," he said, and sympathised when I told him I longed to leave home.

"Wish I could offer you one of my flats," he said. "Trouble is they're controlled. I can't give my tenants notice, but if one leaves you'll get first refusal. That's a promise."

I thanked him for his kindness, but gave up hope soon afterwards when Mr. Edgar retired. Would he remember me?

Months passed and my health deteriorated further with a suspected duodenal ulcer and other internal troubles. I was under hospital observation and went every month for a check-up. One day the specialist looked at me thoughtfully.

"You are not responding to treatment," he said bluntly. "Isn't it time you told me what's upsetting you?"

Something snapped inside me and I burst into floods of tears. Slowly the story came out, how my father never spoke to me, the death of my brother during the war and the tension at home. I did not tell him of my association with the Exclusive Brethren, with all its attendant restrictions and rules. Had I done so he would undoubtedly have advised me to leave them.

"If you value your health you must leave home at once," he insisted. "When you come next month I want to hear that you have moved. Otherwise you might as well not see me. I can do little for you until you remove the cause of this inner tension."

Lillian had hardly opened the door that evening before I poured out my troubles.

"I *must* find a flat or bed-sitter . . . anything," I blurted out.

"I've been thinking about you," Lillian replied calmly. "You know, it may be that God won't lead you to another home just because you *want* to go. He will move you when you really *need* to go," she said.

"But I *do* need to now, the doctor says it's urgent," I replied.

"Then the Great Physician knows all about your case. Leave it to Him," Lillian advised.

I envied her peace and assurance. Impatience and fretting had become second nature to me. I knew all the stock phrases like "If you worry you do not trust. If you trust you do not worry." But I just did not know how to stop worrying and trust God more fully. In fact I was positively alarmed when Lillian suggested that God might not move me at all. He could give me the grace and strength to rise above the friction and coldness.

"Be willing to stay and be strengthened where you are," Lillian urged.

She really got through to me with that advice. Suddenly I was willing. I ceased struggling and yielded myself to God, laying everything at His feet. That night I slept soundly—deep, refreshing sleep that I had not known for months. I was still at peace on the following Friday when I had a telephone call at the office. It was from Mr. Edgar.

"Still looking for a flat?" he asked.

"Y-yes," I faltered.

"Well, one of mine's vacant. The old girl cleared out yesterday. Glad to see her go, I can get the place cleaned up now. Come and see it tomorrow. If you like it, it's yours. Rent's controlled, you'll afford it all right."

The 'phone slipped from my grasp and I felt sick.

"What's up?" asked the clerk at the next desk.

"That was Mr. Edgar, he's offered me a flat. I don't want to live in Brighton though, do I?"

"Why not?" asked the clerk. "You've belly-ached long enough about finding a place. I should have thought an igloo in Greenland wasn't to be sneezed at."

That decided me. Why shouldn't I live in Brighton? Mr. Edgar had travelled to London daily after he bought the flats. If he could do it, so could I.

My heart thumped as I rang Mr. Edgar's doorbell. He welcomed me into the large house divided into five flats and led the way to the door at the far end of the spacious hall.

"Your front door, dear," he said, flinging it open.

I stepped into a huge bed-sitting room and loved it on sight. I loved the view from the bay window, too—tall trees across the valley all bronze and burnished gold in the autumn sun. The kitchen shared the same view. I explored the bathroom and toilet and was delighted that they overlooked next door's rose garden.

"It's marvellous!" I exclaimed.

That was the first of several week-end trips to Brighton. I arranged for the flat to be redecorated, and had the time of my life buying the furnishings. Mr. Edgar 'phoned me when everything had been delivered. I packed immediately and my landlord proudly showed me into my new home.

I looked at the roaring fire he had kindly lit, then my eyes gazed mistily at the beige carpet patterned in orange and green, and the three piece suite in the same shade of green. I blinked at the medium oak table and chairs, the bed tucked away in the far corner and the oak wardrobe to match. To hide my tears I went to the window and looked out, my fingers caressing the oatmeal curtains boldly patterned in green, brown, orange and yellow.

My dream had come true. Here indeed was home sweet home.

Chapter 8

HEARTBREAKINGS AND SEARCHINGS

THE BRETHREN KNEW NOTHING of my move. My request for a letter of commendation to the Brighton Assembly took a leading Surrey brother completely by surprise. I waited, but no letter came. Instead a car load of brothers arrived one evening to express their concern at my secret departure.

They rebuked me for not confiding in them and emphasized our unity in Christ. After I had shown due contrition for my independence, one of the brothers fetched a hamper from the car. They then all settled down to a picnic supper round my fire. Before they left the brothers requested me to fetch a hat, so that they could commend me to the Lord in prayer before leaving. (A brother will not pray in the presence of a sister unless her head is covered.)

I later learned that if I had received those brothers' rebuke in a rebellious spirit, they would not have felt "free" to eat in my flat, but would have had their meal by the roadside.

I can only put my silent departure down to my weariness at being watched and criticised. Subconsciously I wanted to escape from the Exclusive Brethren, yet such was their stranglehold that, even though I was in a new district, I felt bound to link up with the local Assembly. When the letter of commendation came

I did not immediately contact them. Part of me wanted to do so immediately but another part rebelled. Yet where else could I go for Christian fellowship? A large Anglican church nearby looked inviting but how could I attend a place "so steeped in error"? Eventually guilt and loyalty drove me to the Exclusive Assembly.

The Brighton "Saints" were less learned but more legal than those in Surrey. They eyed me critically and soon acquainted me with their rigid views. These were exactly the opposite of those of the Surrey Brethren.

"It is unseemly for a young woman to live alone," they asserted. "You should be with your parents."

I explained that they were not Christians, but this made no difference. They insisted that I was exposing myself to grave fleshly temptations. Several local brothers called uninvited, but my landlord stopped their nosiness by refusing them entrance. Soon I was labelled a "weak sister in need of help" but took no notice. Next my clothes were censured.

"In the Bible red is symbolic of prostitution," a staid old brother said. "Consider Rahab, the harlot, who hung a scarlet cord in her window."

"In Proverbs a virtuous woman is commended for clothing her household in scarlet," I countered. "She was no prostitute, her husband was a leading man in the city."

A more "subject" sister would not have answered back. My reply so shocked the old brother that he hopped from one foot to the other in agitation. His main concern was that I should bow to the will of the Brethren.

Pressure increased and other brothers reproved me for wearing a red hat, gloves and shoes. I was also reproved for wearing a gold locket and chain. A brother who invited me home to tea glared at it with disapproval. That locket, and my preference for wearing red, provided him with the ideal opportunity to read me Paul's words to Timothy: "I will . . . that women adorn themselves in modest apparel . . . and sobriety; not with . . . gold or pearls . . ." (1 Timothy 2: 8, 9).

I still did not consider it immodest to wear red. As a girl in my twenties I hated the dull colours worn by other sisters. I was determined not to copy them, but heads shook sadly at my wilfulness. As for the locket, the fact that it was gold was of no significance. To me its value was sentimental, since it contained a miniature photograph of my brother, who died in the war. I told my Exclusive accuser that the wearing of one small locket and chain could hardly be described as "adorning oneself with gold", but he would not agree.

"It is more than enough," he declared, and told me that a saintly brother in Hove would not even allow his wife to wear a gold wedding ring. He had one specially made of platinum for her.

"Well, it won't stop me wearing this locket when I feel like it," I countered, and the brother pursed his lips disapprovingly.

Had I been brought up among the Exclusive Brethren such insubjection would have been knocked out of me in childhood. If I had belonged to a close-knit, affectionate Exclusive family (and I knew of many), then loyalty to my parents would have reduced me to meek submissiveness.

In spite of this bad start some of the sisters were very kind to me and I made several friends. I felt specially drawn to Mrs. Hammond, who had a "weak background" and whose husband worshipped in the Church of England. She was a motherly woman and I appreciated the way she took me under her wing. One day she gave me a book but asked me not to tell the Brethren. It was called *The Christian's Secret of a Happy Life* by Hannah Pearsall Smith—a Quaker. I still treasure that book, but cannot express how much it meant to me at the time. A bad habit of mine is to turn to the end of a book before reading it. On the last page of this one I read:

When I feel the cold, I can say, "He sends it,"
  And His wind blows blessing, I surely know;
For I've never a want but that He attends it;
  And my heart beats warm, though the winds may blow.
The soft sweet summer was warm and glowing,
  Bright were the blossoms on every bough;
I trusted Him when the roses were blowing,
  I trust Him now.

Small were my faith should it weakly falter,
  Now that the roses have ceased to blow;
Frail were the trust that now should alter,
  Doubting His love when the storm-clouds grow.
If I trust Him once I must trust Him ever,
  And His way is best, though I stand or fall,
Through wind or storm He will leave me never,
  For He sends all.

Tears streamed down my face as I read. Did I relate these verses to the Bible Study days in Clive's house when learning made the world seem warm and glowing and bright? Or did I, perhaps, sense storm clouds brewing that would cast me wholly upon God? I cannot say, but the words moved me deeply. Certainly I did not dream that one day they would mean infinitely more to me.

So much of that book met my need that I am certain God moved Mrs. Hammond to buy it for me. Doubts and misgivings rose to the surface and grew stronger as I read:

"Many earnest and honest-hearted children of God have been deluded into paths of extreme fanaticism, while all the while thinking they were closely following the Lord. God, who sees the sincerity of their hearts, can and does, I am sure, pity and forgive. . . ."

Why, I wondered, had God allowed me to join the Exclusive Brethren if it was all a ghastly mistake? He knew my sincerity and earnestness. My motives had been the best.

Mrs. Hammond listened sympathetically when I confided my anxious doubts. She admitted that her own loyalties were divided between her family, who were all Brethren, and her husband, who could not stand Exclusive dogmatism and legality.

"Why didn't God stop me? I could have been doing useful Christian work. I'm wasting time here!" I blurted out.

"The Lord never enforces His will or way on us," Mrs. Hammond replied. "He gave us free will, but if you did choose wrong, my dear, I'm sure He will lead you back into the right way."

"Lead me into the right way!" I thought with pounding heart. "Away from this By-Path Meadow and back to the King's highway."

"No, the Lord does not wash His hands of us when we go wrong," Mrs. Hammond continued. "Perhaps He has something for you to do among us before you move on."

I longed to be useful, to practise Christianity instead of always learning about it. Before long I found I was not the only "weak sister". Several others were lonely and discouraged through lack of fellowship. The harsh judgment they received did much to dispel my idealistic picture of the Brethren. I determined to help these sisters. God loved them, and I wanted to show them love too. Accordingly I invited first one, then another "weak sister" to my flat. Their appreciation was touching. Mavis came first and it was a pleasure to see how eagerly she reached forward to warm her hands at my roaring fire.

"Can't remember when I last felt so welcome, luv," she said with enthusiasm, and I felt privileged to share her burdens and sorrows.

Mavis was an unmarried mother who had lost her daughter through malnutrition some years previously. Before the child's birth Mavis was excommunicated, but later restored to fellowship after due repentance; she had been cold-shouldered ever since.

I still have the plastic pegs that Mavis gave me. Tears glistened in her eyes when she handed them to me and I felt a lump in my throat. Mavis earned a meagre living by selling clothes pegs, tramping miles in leaky shoes in all weather. It appalled me that her child had died because she was ostracised even by her own parents when she desperately needed food and shelter. I turned to Christ's words to the woman taken in adultery and found no condemnation there, only compassion. How could men who professed to follow Christ be so heartless?

At last I could see that Christianity *must* take a practical form. It consists of far more than Bible study and eloquent sermons on Sundays. Surely the Christ who heard my prayers as a child wanted to reach Mavis too?

I faced a dilemma. What should I do? Remain in fellowship with these modern Pharisees or withdraw? If I left, how could I help the "weaker" sisters? I spent sleepless nights searching for the answer but had not found it when I met Priscilla.

Priscilla was about thirty, and I was delighted when she came to tea. She never visited any Brethren or even talked to them after meetings. She locked herself in her room for hours on end and was on the brink of a mental breakdown. It took some persuasion to get Priscilla to tea. At first she sat twisting her handkerchief nervously but soon relaxed in the armchair and gazed into the fire. I never tried to force her confidence, but let her know she was welcome to come whenever she pleased.

When Priscilla did confide in me I listened in shocked silence to her bitter, heart-rending story.

"I never pray and often doubt the existence of God," she told me. "If He exists, He is no God of love."

Priscilla had been brought up under the harshest discipline: no games or dolls (her father considered them idols), and no books except Bible stories. She was forbidden to play with "worldly" children and missed much schooling through ill-health.

"You've never lived," I thought sadly, and when I remembered the wild, free holidays of my own childhood it shamed me that I had ever felt sorry for myself.

Priscilla was so broken in body and spirit that it was

useless to apply my own solution to her problem. She could not leave home to recover her health, being incapable of work or fending for herself. She was the victim of a tyrannical system that stopped at nothing to enforce "separation from the world". It amazed me that a woman of her age could have remained so isolated. She told me that she had never seen a woman's magazine at close range until she came to my flat. I laughingly threw a copy of *Woman's Own* on to her lap but she swept it away like a viper.

"Don't tempt me!" she cried. "Father said such papers are instruments of the Devil. It would have a terrible hold once I began to read."

Poor Priscilla, I often wonder what became of her. The little I could do was so inadequate, yet I like to think that by staying among the Brethren I brought a little sunshine into her drab, mixed-up life.

It would take too long to tell of all the "misfits" who came to my flat but I believe Mrs. Hammond was right when she said God had a job for me to do. He wanted me to give when I could—hospitality and love.

Word went round about the sisters I entertained and the Brethren called my flat the Cave of Adullam. This meant little to me until I read how King David escaped to this cave. He was joined by everyone who was discontented, in debt or in distress. It made me smile.

In addition to the weak sisters in the meeting, I was also wayward enough to make some outside friends. My closest friend was Beryl, whom I met on the train. Through her I got to know Gillian and Marion and we made a daily foursome on the 8.13 to Victoria. Many a laugh shortened the journey. Once a seat collapsed, depositing a smart city gentleman on the floor. He muttered something inaudible when helped up, then buried himself behind *The Financial Times*. We were glad he did as none of us could keep a straight face.

Another day a frail-looking lady asked a stout fellow-passenger to move her dog from the only vacant seat.

"Certainly not, I've paid for him!" the stout woman snapped.

"I've paid too, and I'm tired," the frail traveller argued.

"Well, my dog's tired!"

A heated argument followed that must have exhausted both women. The dog slumbered peacefully on.

I loved the Saturdays when these three friends came to tea and chattered non-stop. We also went on country walks together, but I enjoyed my walks with Beryl most. She re-kindled my childhood love of nature and I pondered anew the beauty and wonder of God's creation. Beryl knew the name of every bird that sang and every wayside flower. I still thrill to the memory of a link fence we passed. Tufted vetch covered it in a beautiful curtain of bluish-purple flowers. The bees appreciated that vetch more than we did and it fascinated us to watch them buzz from flower to flower.

Beryl was, and is still, a very modest person. Several months passed before she told me she had written two books. She lent them to me and every page revealed her love and reverence for nature. She has a gift of painting pictures with words—delightful sunset scenes, bluebell woods, shady lanes where primroses bloom. I particularly love Beryl's poem "A Sprig of Rosemary", which typifies her quiet, reflective personality. She lets me tip-toe beside her to share a delightful reverie:

"There's rosemary, that's for remembrance"—yes . . ."

> *I remember the steps, and the lonely gate,*
>   *The slabbed roof, mossy and brown,*
> *And the whitewashed walls with their hollyhocks,*
>   *And the jessamine trailing down.*
> *I remember the well with its fern-fringed flags,*
>   *The water butt painted blue,*
> *And the windows wide to the downland air,*
>   *And the sunlight slanting through.*
>
> *I remember the path where the seafogs cling,*
>   *The thyme in the sun-parched grass.*
> *And the gentle slopes where the sheep-bells ring*
>   *As the slow sheep quietly pass . . .*
> *I remember the sign-post, crooked and grey,*
>   *(Five miles to the town, no less)*
> *The view o'er the weald, and the blue-rimmed bay . . .*
>   *"Rosemary, that's for remembrance" . . . yes.*

Because of Beryl I, too, love that old water butt. With her I catch the scent of the jessamine trailing down.

On one country walk we came to a pond covered in duckweed. I poked about for newts and caught a baby frog. It reminded me of a family of little frogs I found in a ditch when I was a child.

"They hopped everywhere," I said, "and I wanted to take some home as company for my pet frog Bog-eyes. I emptied some sticky toffees out of a bag into my pocket, then popped a dozen baby frogs into the bag."

"I hope you didn't have far to go," Beryl chided.

"No, and I ran most of the way," I assured her. "Bog-eyes was sitting under his usual rock so I tipped the little frogs into the pond in front of him," I went on. "They swam to the edge and climbed out, and to my horror Bog-eyes ate the lot. I tried to rescue one whose back legs stuck out of his mouth but, with another gulp, he disappeared head first."

After relating this tragedy, Beryl suddenly turned to me and said, "Have you ever thought of writing, Christine? I'm sure you could if you tried."

"Writing what?" I asked.

"Nature articles," she suggested.

This brief conversation proved another milestone in my life. Beryl brought to light a love of writing long stifled by the Exclusive Brethren. That evening I wrote an article for the *Sussex Magazine* and was overjoyed when the Editor accepted it. A literary career had begun! The rejection slips that followed did not deter me, and another article in the *Kent and Sussex Journal* spurred me on. I regarded my rejections as "experience gained".

Beryl encouraged me when the going was hard, and it is to her that I owe any success I have achieved.

The Brethren saw me with Beryl and disapproved of our friendship. Had they known of my articles they would have disapproved of those too. But I was safe there because the Brethren never read magazines. How strongly they felt about "worldly literature" was brought home to me through an incident in Preston Park, Brighton.

Neither of my parents showed much interest when I moved to Brighton. I had gone a fortnight before my father asked where I was. Perhaps he had not missed me until then! But my mother wrote regularly and I think my letters meant more to her than I had expected.

I tried to persuade her to come and see my flat, but she was afraid of being caught in a fog. She came the following spring and was surprised to find me living so comfortably. She stayed the week-end and on Saturday we sat in the park enjoying the scent of roses. While we were there I read her *The Wind in the Willows.* As I read a shadow fell across the page and a voice startled me.

"Are you reading something profitable to your soul?"

Dumbfounded, I looked into the accusing eyes of a fanatical brother in his early thirties.

"And what about your companion, is she a believer in the Lord Jesus?" he demanded.

"This is my mother and I'm reading her a nature book," I said.

He tried to take it from me, but I snapped the book shut and put it behind my back. We stared each other out and he eventually walked away.

"What was all that about?" my mother asked, but I was too angry to explain. It would have been unwise anyway as she disliked my being an Exclusive sister.

That Sunday my mother cooked the dinner while I went to the Morning Meeting. I was still furious and determined to tell that brother to mind his own business. To my frustration only his wife was there. I went out of my way to walk home with her after the meeting, bent on telling her what I thought of her husband.

On the way she confided that she lived in constant dread of having another baby. She already had five children under six years of age. Our eyes met, hers haunted and darkly undercircled, and my anger changed to pity.

"Isn't there something you could do about it?" I asked vaguely.

"My husband won't allow it. He says we must have as many children as the Lord sends," she replied helplessly.

On hearing that I despised her husband even more, but said nothing. The poor girl looked so worn out that she obviously had enough to put up with. I went home to dinner thankful that I was not married. A week later I became involved in my one and only love affair among the Brethren!

I was attracted to Timothy from the first time he spoke to me, and romance blossomed quickly. Tim had a motorbike, even though the Brethren thought it devilish, and I liked him the more for that. I loved riding pillion, with the wind blowing through my long pony-tail. (I screwed my hair into a respectable bun on Sundays.) Life was great! We sped round the countryside and climbed the Downs. Hand in hand, we sat on Ditchling Beacon watching the sun sinking like a great tired balloon and Tim kissed me passionately. We listened to the wind whispering in the wheat, the softest, sweetest music I had ever heard. For supper we ate toasted crumpets in my flat, and no manna could have tasted more heavenly. It was wonderful to feel loved and cherished and I responded with all my heart.

Tim's father was a wealthy and influential brother in a neighbouring meeting. He loved money and parted with as little as possible, but he did promise Tim the price of a house when he married. That was before Tim met me. When our romance became known, Tim's parents went into my credentials. I was far too "unsound" to be considered and they were determined to separate us. Their son was to marry a sister with a good Brethren pedigree.

Tim was greatly distressed by his parents' opposition and I was heartbroken. He faced moral blackmail. Tim had little money and his father refused the promised house unless he married a sister of whom *he* approved.

Tim detested the hypocrisy and much else that went on among the Brethren but, like many Brethren children, fear of parental disfavour was his Achilles heel. His moment of truth came when his parents rejected me. I feared for our future and for Tim. Would he break free and act for himself, or for ever be crushed into submission by dominating parents? Who would win?

I waited in anguish. This was Tim's battle. If he lost, I was lost too! He put up a good fight, and for a time my hopes soared, only to be finally dashed to the ground. Timothy gave me up, and slunk off a defeated man.

My wounded heart took a long time to heal. I tried to convince myself I had escaped a life of bondage, but it did not cure the loneliness. Tim had aroused a deep longing for someone to love and care for. I wanted to be one with the man of God's choice and had believed Tim would be my partner. Sadder and wiser, must I now resign myself to being an old maid?

The temptation to leave the Brethren was strong, but just then a young brother "fell by the wayside". His case came up in the Care Meeting and many heads shook sadly over his withdrawal from the Assembly.

"Our brother has fallen into Satan's clutches!" a leading brother boomed in warning tones. "Yes, Satan's clutches, and who can tell what his end will be? Destruction of body and soul, that's the devil's work. . . ."

I cringed in my seat in silent misery. This would be my fate, too, if I deliberately turned my back on the "light"—or left the Brethren. And so cowardice continued to keep me in my place week by week, outwardly a conformer but a rebel at heart.

Chapter 9

THE FETTERS FALL

THE AUTUMN after my broken romance a new accountancy clerk, Geoffrey Wood, came to Electra House. I knew him by sight and had admired his black, wavy hair, but had never spoken to him. A few weeks later another clerk told me that I had missed a treat by not going to the staff Christmas party.

"That chap Wood stood at the door and kissed all the girls goodbye," the clerk said, grinning from ear to ear.

This scrap of gossip did not interest me much, but the following spring I pricked up my ears when the same clerk burst into my office with the latest news.

"You'll never guess what, that Wood got converted over the weekend. You and he should get on fine," he told me.

"What do you mean, converted?" I asked cautiously.

"You know—SAVED!" the clerk said, for to him it was a huge joke. "It happened at All Souls in Langham Place. Ask him yourself if you don't believe me. He can't stop talking about it. One thing though, he won't kiss the girls any more now he's turned holy!"

I was so thrilled that I wanted to rush off and tell Geoffrey Wood how pleased I was. One thing held me back. The Brethren had recently intensified their teaching on "separation". I was already under pressure because of my association with Beryl and Marion. So strong was the "purge" that even I had twinges of guilt.

They were not strong enough to make me give up these two friends but I appeased my conscience with the assurance that I would form no more "worldly links".

Geoffrey Wood upset my resolution and I became greatly disturbed about the Exclusive path I followed. Brethren teaching apart, surely God wanted me to speak to this new-born Christian? The angels in heaven were rejoicing over him. Couldn't I join in?

What was the right thing to do? The problem assumed such proportions that it became a test of loyalty to the Brethren. Either I would go on more whole-heartedly with them, or break away and talk to whom I chose. To anyone unfamiliar with Exclusive fetters it must be hard to understand how this simple matter could have caused such heart-searching. I had become more of a slave to their rigid system than I realised and it alarmed me.

I was still undecided whether to speak to him or not, when Geoffrey Wood paused in the office corridor to hold a swing door open for me. That moment I knew I *must* speak to him. It would be unchristian not to. But my courage failed and I shot through the door with scarcely a Thank You.

"The next time you *will* speak to that man," I thought.

A few days later the opportunity came when we waited for the lift together. I opened my mouth but the words froze on my lips and we ascended in silence. I hated myself for it, and hated the loyalty to the Brethren that had struck me dumb.

"You're doing what the Brethren want you to and not what the Lord wants," I told myself, yet failed to recognise the full truth of this.

Next time there was no escape. Geoffrey Wood

walked towards me as I went out to lunch. I took a deep breath and plunged in.

"Excuse me, but I hear you've recently become a Christian. I'm so pleased," I said.

His whole face glowed with pleasure and I knew that I had done the right thing. Geoffrey told me how lonely he had been that Sunday night. He had wandered from his "digs" not knowing where to go or what to do. At Oxford Circus a girl out "fishing" for All Souls handed him a card inviting him to the service.

"Where's the church?" he asked.

She pointed to it and off he hurried. The Rev. John Stott preached on the woman at Sychar's well that evening. Before the service ended, the Saviour who had touched that woman's sinful heart had touched Geoffrey's heart, too.

We had so much to say to each other, but Geoffrey's lunch-hour was over. He asked me where I worked and I told him I had my own office on the fourth floor. He became a daily visitor and we discussed many things. Inevitably it came out that I was an Exclusive sister. Geoffrey had never even heard of the Exclusive Brethren and the implications were lost on him. He invited me to spend a Sunday with him.

"I'll take you to All Souls," he said eagerly. "I'd like you to meet the Rev. John Stott."

My refusal puzzled him.

"How can it be wrong to meet such a grand Christian? It doesn't make sense," Geoffrey asked.

How humbling that a "babe" in Christ had more insight than I had! My explanation did not help much, but I made a counter-offer and invited Geoffrey to Brighton. He set off on his bicycle early Sunday morning and arrived just in time for a wash and brush up before the Morning Meeting.

I felt sorry for him sitting all alone behind that wretched board, but worse followed. At the close of the meeting an elder brother stood at the door to shake "the elect" by the hand. I introduced Geoffrey as a new Christian and he came forward with a friendly smile and outstretched hand.

"I'm not free to shake hands with you," the brother said stiffly, "but I trust the meeting has led you into more light."

The light went from Geoffrey's smile and his hand fell limply to his side. I stumbled out of the hall angry, ashamed and baffled. Surely the Brethren could at least take an interest in those who came seeking the truth! But they had "separation" under their skins so much that they were no longer concerned. Geoffrey said that the brother had looked at him with nothing but cold suspicion and he was deeply hurt. For me it was the beginning of the end.

* * * *

A FEW WEEKS later my landlord died of a heart attack. All his tenants loved him and were greatly distressed. I could not believe that I would not hear him singing any more as he shaved. I still listened for his 7 a.m. thump on my front door, but it never came. Mr. Edgar had been a real father to me, the only father I had known, and his passing left an aching void in my heart.

Mrs. Edgar went away after the funeral and everything changed. My flat lost its charms and I was heartily sick of the Exclusive Brethren. I had nothing against my personal friends among them, and loved my "second

Mum", Mrs. Hammond, as much as ever. I could not even blame them for being Exclusive. They did not regard themselves as ensnared in any way and I almost envied them. They were the lucky ones, possessing a true piety and a simple sincerity that asked no questions. I was the odd one out who could no longer accept rules and regulations without probing the whys and where-fores. It was the tyrannical system which I hated, not individuals.

I sought Beryl's company more than ever. Her quiet spirit was a balm to my troubled one. Without her friendship in Brighton and Geoffrey's in London, life would have been bleak indeed.

Geoffrey never again came to a Brethren meeting with me. He told me that he had to look at me as a person, separating me in his mind from the people I was connected with. Otherwise our friendship would have to end. I panicked, realising how much Geoffrey's friendship meant to me. He was so happy, intelligent and warm hearted that I dreaded losing his companion-ship. Without realising it, because this time it was a slower process, I was already falling in love with him.

To my joy, Geoffrey still cycled to Brighton to see me, but always on a Saturday. We also spent happy evenings together in town when he was not at night school. We became very close friends and he often said he wished I lived nearer.

"Why don't you come back to Surrey?" he asked.

I was already toying with the idea and his suggestion spurred me into action. I paid one of my rare week-end visits to my parents with the idea of looking round for a flat. On my way to their house I saw a new block of flats. I was so excited that I jumped off the bus and ran back to the site. To my disappointment they were all sold, but the foreman told me that another block would soon be built down the side-road. He advised me to see the Estate Agent immediately as flats close to the station sold quickly.

My intention had been to rent a flat—but why not buy one? A mortgage would probably cost no more than rent, and in the end I would have something to show for my money. I hurried to the Estate Agent and asked to see the plans of the new block.

"They're the same design as those on the main road, but have the advantage of facing south," the agent explained.

"I should like this centre one with the bay window," I said boldly. "Will you please reserve it for me?"

I was so ignorant about buying property that I knew next to nothing about deposits, mortgages and surveyors' fees; but I soon learned. The deposit required was no worry because I had always been thrifty and could use the money I had saved in Brighton. The mortgage was the problem. The agent said that he could probably arrange one, but I politely refused, preferring to make my own arrangements.

First one Building Society turned me down, then another, and I soon discovered that single women were regarded unfavourably. I was so determined to get a mortgage from one society that I applied to two branches and finally direct to the Head Office, only to be refused each time. I hated admitting defeat but eventually went back to the agent and told him that I did not see how I could have the flat after all, as it was impossible to get a mortgage. He repeated his initial offer of arranging one and this time I accepted eagerly.

He got me a mortgage from the very Society that had turned me down three times! Obviously I had not pulled the right strings.

After my first visit to the agent I could hardly wait for Monday to come. I went to work early in the hope of seeing Geoffrey. He overtook me on Waterloo Bridge and I excitedly told him my news.

"I've bought a flat in Surbiton," I said and expected him to be pleased.

He did not say much then but later, when the mortgage came through, he said he wished I had not bought the flat.

"Why?" I asked.

"Because I want to marry you and it would have been super to choose a place together," he said.

"Do you realise the Brethren would sling me out if I married you? My friend married an Anglican and, although she's back in fellowship now, she's never lived down the disgrace," I said tactlessly.

"Do those Brethren mean so much more to you than I do?" Geoffrey asked disappointedly.

He took my hand in his and looked at me questioningly. In that moment I knew I loved him. Here was the partner I had longed for. No one must keep us apart. Geoffrey wanted us to become engaged immediately and begged me to give up the Exclusive Brethren.

"Please give me time," I hedged. "I can't just walk out after all these years. I've got to think things out."

"Well, pack them up when you leave Brighton and we'll become engaged then," Geoffrey suggested. "You'll soon feel at home at All Souls. They're a grand crowd."

I was not happy about this. How could I return to

Surrey and cast aside the friends who had once meant so much to me? All the same, I still marvel at Geoffrey's patience, understanding and tolerance.

At last the flat was ready. Exactly four years after I had moved away I returned to Surrey. My new home was delightfully sunny and bright and Geoffrey helped me to get it straight. He made pelmets, put up shelves and curtains and laid the carpets. Watching him, I thought wistfully how wonderful it would be if we were already married and life had no problems. The silly thing is that we *could* have been married, but my misguided sense of loyalty hindered that.

I got into touch with the Brethren again, and my friends greeted me with genuine pleasure. But Geoffrey was hurt because he had expected me to leave them. I was hurt too, but for a different reason. My letter of commendation from the Brighton Brethren was anything but flattering. The harder I tried to be loyal, the less they thought of me. That letter had its advantages though—it helped to loosen the fetters that bound me.

In November Geoffrey and I became engaged, but secretly as far as the Brethren were concerned. I chose a ring with a ruby set between two diamonds, the ruby to remind me of the virtuous woman in the last chapter of Proverbs, whom I hoped to emulate. I slipped the ring off before attending Brethren meetings. Call it cowardice if you will, but I dreaded becoming involved in endless arguments over my pending marriage. Although I was slow to shake off the fetters, I was determined to marry the man who loved me and whom I loved dearly. If I was not good enough for an Exclusive marriage, the Brethren were not coming between me and an "outside" Christian!

Chapter 10

ESCAPE

DESPITE MY DETERMINATION to marry the man of my heart, as the year drew to a close I became more and more on edge. We had planned to marry in the spring, after Geoffrey had taken his accountancy exams. Sensing my tension, he brought the date forward to January.

"No more Brethren for you when we're married," he teased. "We'll worship together at All Souls."

I was not ready for such a drastic change and it increased the tension. My feelings were so mixed that I hardly knew what I did want. Where would the wedding take place anyway?

"Ours can't be a Brethren wedding," I said, "and I wouldn't want it to be, but we can't be married in a church either, can we?"

Geoffrey would have liked a church wedding but agreed it had its problems. Neither his father nor my parents took any interest in our engagement and did not wish to come to our wedding. Geoffrey's father had too many troubles of his own to bother about us. As for my parents, why should they be interested? My father was a stranger. My mother took the line that, since I had left home to make my own life, why should she put herself out? I could see her point of view and accepted it.

Still the question remained—where should we marry?

It would have to be a quiet wedding, private too. I would look ridiculous walking down the aisle of an empty church, quite apart from my uneasy conscience over a "church" wedding. Much as I wanted to, I still could not shake the Exclusive shackles off. Christmas was almost upon us before we reached a decision.

"Let's talk things over with John Stott," Geoffrey suggested. "He'll help you to free yourself from the Exclusives too."

"How can a rector help me? He'll know nothing about Exclusive Brethren," I argued.

How wrong I was! From the experienced way he spoke to me when I went to see him, the Rev. John Stott must have "sorted out" many other Exclusives, and I recall with gratitude his tact and understanding. I had felt sick all day at the alarming prospect of talking to an Anglican minister, but his winsome smile soon put me at ease.

"I want to leave the Exclusive Brethren, but feel I'm being disloyal," I confessed. "There's a lot of weakness and failure among them, and I've failed too, but I feel I'll have sunk even lower if I desert them altogether."

He went to the root of the matter by asking whom I was trying to please. Was I walking before men, or was my eye on Christ, who said: "Follow me"? John Stott showed me, in the nicest possible way, that I had been walking in bondage—obeying God's laws (as defined by the Exclusive Brethren) from *fear* of judgment. As a daughter of God, it was my privilege to do His will because I *loved* Him, not out of a sense of duty. He showed me that my whole attitude had become one of legality and suggested that it was high time to walk in liberty. I was completely convinced by the verse he referred to. It became a staff to help me on my way: "Stand fast therefore in the liberty wherewith Christ hath made us free, and be not entangled again with the yoke of bondage" (Galatians 5: v. 1).

I went home light of heart and with the words "be not entangled again" ringing through my head. The Exclusive Brethren could hold me no longer. I had finished with them!

So, at last, I escaped from By-Path Meadow and returned to the King's highway. What a weighty burden of legality and dogmatism I left behind at that happy milestone! When I told Geoffrey of my decision he wept tears of joy. It was only then that I fully realised how the fetters that had bound me had been hurting him too.

Would I have had the courage to take that step but for him? I have since heard of Exclusive brothers and sisters who have "come out" but have been completely lost. Suddenly they feel like fish out of water. The power that has for so long gripped them is no longer there. One ex-sister confided to me that for a while she felt utterly lost and helpless. A long time passed before she could make a firm decision about anything. She had been so used to having her mind made up for her.

I admire brothers and sisters who "come out"; it costs them far more than it cost me. They are disowned by relatives and friends for life. I heard of a brother who had a nervous breakdown under the strain, while yet another collapsed and died. I mention this to show how great is the stranglehold and how utterly one is rejected. Ex-Exclusives suffer financially, too, since parents disinherit children who forsake the fellowship. But this is a minor consideration compared with the emotional upheaval and heartbreak. I was fortunate, I had no close ties—and a good man to support me. All the same, final correspondence with the Brethren distressed me. Their official "withdrawal letter" read:

> *"Dear Mrs. Wood,*
> *It is with great sorrow of heart that I have to inform you that, at the meeting of assembly character held last evening (of which you were advised) it was decided that, in view of the mixed marriage you have now contracted with one not walking in the light of Paul's ministry (to whom was committed the light of the assembly), we can no longer walk with you. For your information the scriptures read and considered were: Nehemiah 13. 23-29 and 2 Timothy 2. 19-22.*
> *Yours faithfully,"*

Geoffrey and I dismissed that letter as rubbish, but I felt strongly about other letters written to me at the time. One brother who wrote had reproached me years before on another matter. My mother had taken me to Switzerland to make up for the holidays we missed during the war. This brother rebuked me severely for having gone.

"Your holiday pandered to the flesh," he asserted. "You have been abroad to see the scenery—the fallen world. You should be dead to all that and walk in the spirit."

This flabbergasted me since I was unaware at the time that the Brethren were not supposed to indulge themselves in admiring the beauties of nature.

"When I go abroad," this brother went on virtuously, "I go to see the Lord's people, not the sinful cities that man has made, or the scenery."

I shrank from this brother's smug attitude. Soon after my marriage the Brethren had a "moral purge". I was given details by a sympathetic sister who secretly kept in touch with me. Many brothers and sisters came under "conviction of sin" at a special meeting and made some revealing confessions. My former accuser confessed that his trips abroad had been to visit women in no way connected with the Lord's people!

Because he displayed a repentant spirit, this brother was not even "withdrawn from". It made me think—and completed my disillusionment.

Not that I was the only one who faced disillusionment. Some time after I had left the Exclusive Brethren, over two thousand brothers and sisters withdrew in protest against "new light" put out by the late James Taylor. This "light" caused so much distress and disruption of family life that news of it leaked into the national newspapers.

Husbands and wives could no longer eat meals with partners who were not in the Meeting. Children who had not asked for fellowship by the age of twelve were likewise forced to eat alone. Aged "unenlightened" relatives were condemned to similar isolation. Hospitality such as I had known when first attending Exclusive Meetings was a thing of the past. If a brother *did* entertain an outsider seeking the truth, the luckless guest must be given his food at a separate table. More rigid Brethren would not even defile themselves by eating in the same room as anyone not "walking in the light".

I thought sadly of my dear friend Mrs. Hammond. It sickened me to visualise her and her Exclusive daughter eating in the dining room while her kindly Anglican husband ate in solitary confinement in the kitchen.

One sister who left the Exclusive Brethren at this time wrote a full letter of explanation. As well as being sent to the Brethren, this letter was also circulated among others who withdrew with her. I quote an extract only:

> *"Looking for the fruit of the Spirit: love, joy, peace, long-suffering, kindness, goodness, self control—as a result of what is considered 'further light', I see instead only mental cruelty, discourtesy, harshness, slander, immorality, religious fanaticism and persecution, the characteristics of the Pharisee, incitement of hatred of parents, the break-up of the family unit . . . I have been profoundly disturbed by the way many of the Exclusive Brethren have spoken of other Christians in a derogatory way, implying that they are lost, and that we are the ONLY people—the others counting for nothing in God's sight as they seem to in ours. . . . I am appalled by the inhumanity, selfishness, self-righteousness. . . ."*

This sister had the courage to voice and act upon the doubts and misgivings that I had suppressed for so long.

* * * *

HOW I thanked God for sending Geoffrey to rescue me from that Exclusive By-Path! We decided to have a quiet wedding in a Register Office, not because this is how the Exclusive Brethren normally marry, but because it was the simplest way in our particular circumstances. We invited two friends as witnesses, then we drove to London for a weekend honeymoon at the Cumberland Hotel.

On the Sunday we again went to see the Rector of All Souls, Langham Place. Mr. Stott prayed with us and Geoffrey and I pledged our faithfulness to each other before God. I was deeply moved, and know Geoffrey was too, when the Rector prayed for God's blessing upon us. He also gave us a small book of guidance for the newly married and I cherish it still.

We then attended the Evening Service at All Souls and, to my surprise, I enjoyed it. I realised that many Brethren malign and berate a form of worship that they know nothing about. It is mainly hearsay and prejudice.

But Geoffrey and I were through with the Exclusive Brethren. Now we had only our future happiness to which to look forward.

Chapter 11

THE RESTORED YEARS

MARRIAGE! To many girls this paints a rosy picture of a new life filled with thrills, excitement, endless joys to share. All too soon we find that much of the time is taken up with the routine things we knew before. Just as in our single days, there are times when we look round for something useful to occupy us.

Not only was our wedding a quiet one; the first few months of our marriage were quiet too. Geoffrey spent every evening either at night school or at home studying for his exams. I loved watching him filling up page after page with his small, neat handwriting, but I never spoke. That would have interrupted his train of thought.

How could I occupy myself creatively? I remembered the articles written in Sussex and tentatively started writing again, this time for children. I sat on the floor gazing into the fire with pencil and paper ready. Sometimes ideas came quickly, sometimes they eluded me, yet I wrote several children's stories. Most of them were published in annuals or magazines.

Towards the end of Geoffrey's course I spotted an advertisement in a boys' magazine offering a prize for the best serial submitted, to be published next year. A serial? Too lengthy for me! I pushed the magazine aside. Later Geoffrey picked it up, saw the advertisement and asked if I had started yet.

"I couldn't write a serial, it would run into thousands of words," I protested.

"Can I? No I can't," Geoffrey teased. "You've admitted defeat without even trying."

His challenge made me determined to try, but no ideas came. Still Geoffrey studied, often into the small hours long after I had gone to bed. Tough as he was, he looked tired and strained and I worried in case he should fall ill before the exams. Somehow he stuck it out.

"Phew! Now for some relaxation while we await the results," he said.

Geoffrey bought a second-hand tandem and we rode for miles, up hill and down dale, often returning home after dark. It was great fun. Once we rounded a bend on a country road and nearly mowed down what I can only describe as a public rabbit rally! Dozens of rabbits scattered in all directions—and we fell off our tandem!

One week-end we visited the Swannery at Abbotsbury. I wandered fascinated along the reed banks and beside the sedges bordering a huge lake. Something clicked inside my brain and I found what I was looking for—the perfect setting for a boys' story. I wrote a serial about four boys who broke into a swannery to steal swans' eggs.

Now it was my turn to work against the clock. The closing date for the competition rushed towards me. I had the deadline so much on my mind that I even called one of the characters Deadline Dick! Geoffrey, who was a "two-finger expert", helped me type the manuscript and I finally delivered it by hand on the appointed day. To our delight it won first prize.

We did everything together. Geoffrey entered

wholeheartedly into my interests and I tried to do the same with his, though when it came to decorating and carpentry I was very much the unskilled mate.

"You be foreman," Geoffrey would say, which was a tactful way of telling me that I was not much good with a paintbrush, hammer or saw.

The more I got to know Geoffrey, the more I loved him. He was so meticulously careful in all he did, so painstaking. Watching him, I realised how sensitive he was, how deeply he felt about many things. This caring came out in many ways.

We both loved the country and often went rambling together. Geoffrey never set off without a small folding saw in his rucksack. When we came to a tree strangled by ivy he would stop, take out his little saw and cut through the offending creeper. He cared about over-grown footpaths too, and we spent many an hour clearing the footpaths of Surrey. Somehow I never minded being stung by nettles or scratched by brambles. It was all part of Geoffrey's good cause.

One lovely day we climbed over an old stone wall and found ourselves on a mossy path arched by yew and giant laurel bushes. Silence reigned along that vaulted path. No bird sang, no breeze whispered among the laurel leaves. We trod silently, spoke only in whispers, and wondered where the path would lead us. Suddenly it opened out on to a grass bank and before us we saw hundreds of golden daffodils. We stood motionless, hand in hand, awestruck by this sight, so unexpected and so beautiful.

Only one thing marred the loveliness. Many daffodils were choked by brambles, others fought for the daylight among a forest of silver birch and sycamore saplings. I knew exactly what Geoffrey would do. He ran down the bank, saw in hand, and began cutting away the brambles. I wished I had a saw too. I sat on the bank and watched Geoffrey tenderly lifting first one and then another deformed stalk, gently coaxing the flower it bore towards the sunlight—and I loved him for it. Between us we cleared a mountain of brambles that day, dragging them to the side of what was once a vast, daffodil strewn lawn.

We returned many times to Geoffrey's Secret Daffodil Garden, as he called it, and worked for hours clearing away briars and thinning out the saplings. We sat on the bank eating picnic lunches, and overhead a green woodpecker laughed continuously. We laughed too, completely happy in our self-appointed task.

"Geoffrey's doing to those daffodils what he's done for me," I thought one day, as I watched him work. "He's freed me from the fear and legality that strangled and choked, stunting my spiritual life. How wonderful to enjoy the sunshine of the King's highway again!"

Geoffrey sat beside me to rest and wiped the perspiration from his brow. I wanted to share my thoughts with him, but felt too shy. I wish I had told him, he would have appreciated knowing.

At last the results of the exams came through. Geoffrey had passed in all subjects. He did not say much, but his hand trembled as he returned the letter to its envelope. I knew how deeply disappointed he would have been if he had failed.

Because I was still working full-time while Geoffrey studied, I had engaged Mrs. Crouch, a motherly old soul, to do my housework. The little job just suited her. It suited me to have her, too. I hated coming home to chores after a gruelling day in the office. In any event it would have disturbed Geoffrey to have me bustling around while he studied. Mrs. Crouch was delighted when I told her of his success.

"Of course Mr. Wood passed, luv," she said. "They wouldn't 'ave the nerve to fail a gent like 'im."

Geoffrey's success and subsequent promotion brought some changes in our life. I gave up my job at Cable and Wireless and faced the unpleasant task of telling Mrs. Crouch that I would no longer need her services. Fortunately she forestalled me by saying that she could not come much longer because she was moving.

"The Council's offered me a duck of a flat over Chessington way, luv," she told me.

Later Geoffrey and I moved to a maisonette. This time we chose it together! I took a part-time job as Secretary to one of the Directors of *Punch* and loved every minute of it. One often hears about the Perfect Secretary. All I can say is that I had the Perfect Boss. He was one of the kindest and most considerate men I have ever met. It was a joy to work for him, and a joy to visit him and his wife in their delightful Oast House in Kent.

When we moved, Geoffrey felt that it would be a good idea to make a fresh start in our Christian worship and service. He disliked travelling up to All Souls because it meant that we were not supporting a local church. Eventually we settled in an evangelical church, where we received a heart-warming welcome. Oddly enough this church later became the first port of call to many seeking a haven after having left the Exclusive Brethren.

Geoffrey shrank from any kind of public speaking or

teaching but was immensely practical in his Christianity. He was completely reliable as a "backroom boy" at the church. We entertained a lot and gathered a circle of friends round us. If anyone needed help with a motor-cycle that would not start or rooms that needed decorating, Geoffrey was always there.

One of our friends, Brenda, staggered us by saying that she was going to sink her savings in a driving school. She rented premises on the main road, bought a car and employed an instructor. Geoffrey was greatly concerned about this venture and spent many hours advising Brenda on the financial aspects. He also taught her book-keeping and prepared her annual accounts for her. He continued to offer his services freely until she had more cars and more instructors, and the business was firmly established.

Some years Geoffrey and I went to the Christmas House-party at Herne Bay Court. Once the host asked us to lead family worship on Christmas morning. He suggested that I should read the Nativity story from the Bible, then Geoffrey would follow with prayer. He declined and I was sorry because I would have liked us to have done it. I asked Geoffrey to read and said I would lead in prayer. Again he refused because "it was the wrong way round."

Yet it warms my heart to recall the huge bonfire Geoffrey willingly helped to build. We all stood round it on Christmas Eve, singing carols and eating hot-dogs, which he helped to serve. The flames leapt high, adding a warm glow to smiling faces—and no one smiled more happily than Geoffrey. He loved to serve and work unobtrusively behind the scenes, doing everything well.

*　　*　　*　　*

IF ANYONE rejoined the Exclusive brethren after having been "withdrawn from", the Brethren referred to the intervening time as "the years the locusts have eaten". After my departure I thought of my years *among* the Brethren as my wasted, locust-eaten years. I wanted to make up for them by doing useful Christian work, but did not know what to do. When asked to help with a Children's Bible Class held in a gymnasium on Sundays, I agreed eagerly.

In addition to running the class I was expected to arrange outings, as a treat for the children, but exhausting for me. It was a good way of winning the children's friendship and confidence.

A little boy named Freddie came to one of these outings. He was a rebel and I knew that he would cause trouble. Sure enough, when the other children played rounders, Freddie ran off to climb trees. When the others played hide-and-seek, Freddie, in open unconcern, made himself a bow and arrow with the aid of one of his plimsoll laces. He glared when I remonstrated with him.

"Don't see why I should do what you want me to," he said defiantly.

On the way home we came to a meadow carpeted with buttercups. The children wanted to pick some "for Mum" so I opened the gate and let them through—all except Freddie who had already climbed over the gate. I watched the children gather large bunches, apart from Freddie of course. He picked a few buttercups near the hedge, then threw them away. He disappeared into the bushes and I suspected he was birds' nesting. Anger mounted, but Freddie kept stooping too low for birds' nesting. He had me puzzled. Now and then I caught glimpses of him crawling through the hedge. Satisfied that he was not disturbing nesting birds, I left him alone.

Buttercups gathered, I herded the children back into the lane—except Freddie. I called crossly to him, telling him we would miss the train if he did not hurry. He ran towards me with one hand tucked underneath his shabby sweater.

"Here you are, miss," he said, and out came a small bunch of violets.

My impatience vanished. I took them from his sticky hand, touched by the expression on his grubby, eager little face. In that moment I realised that the most precious things in life are seldom found on open display. We find them hidden away in unexpected places.

When I agreed to help with the Bible Class I did not realise how much it would involve. I liked the children, but the job was so time-absorbing! We had teachers' meetings on Tuesday evenings and games in the park on Fridays. They were fun and a good way of getting to know the children, but I begrudged the time I wanted to spend with Geoffrey.

Autumn came and the children were sorry when early darkness prevented our Friday games. I was glad, but my relief proved short-lived. No sooner had the games finished than we began planning and rehearsing a Nativity play which was to be the crowning item of the children's Christmas party. Our efforts would be worthwhile if some of the parents who never attended a church came to see the play and be reminded of what Christmas stood for. If only rehearsals did not demand so much time!

A week before Christmas the Class Leader dropped a small bomb by saying: "It's usual for teachers to give each child in their class a small gift."

"Oh dear, that means fourteen extra presents to rush round for," I inwardly sighed.

In fact a hasty trip to Woolworth's produced the lot. The children were so excited on the Sunday before Christmas that it was hard work holding their attention while I delivered my carefully prepared talk on the True Meaning of Christmas.

"Don't rush off yet," I pleaded at the end of the class. "I've a small present for each of you to open on Christmas Day."

I bestowed crayons, sugar mice, or gold coins with chocolate fillings on each waiting child. I then dismissed them and began packing up. Instead of rushing off as I expected, the children hung back.

"Please, miss, this is for you," said a shrill voice, and little Paula handed me a gaily-wrapped packet. It came as a pleasant surprise when the other children shyly produced small parcels from their pockets, too.

"Open them now," pleaded Sandra.

"Yes, go on, miss," encouraged Freddie.

I sat down and undid the carefully tied gifts and was greatly touched by the contents of those small packets: a handpainted calendar, a carefully sewn comb case, a knitted kettle holder, a raffia mat, and so on.

"You haven't opened m. .my p. .present yet," the fair haired Andrew stuttered.

We unearthed his gift from the pile of wrapping paper and with wide, eager eyes he watched me open it. Inside lay a long wavy piece of red plastic with a mouth and two eyes painted at one end.

"It's a b. .bookmarker. It's meant to b. .be a b. . book-worm," Andrew said, still studying my face anxiously.

Shame filled me as I looked into his clear blue eyes. A reluctant visit to Woolworth's was all I had devoted to my presents. These children had behaved so differently. They had put loving workmanship into their little gifts. In this way they gave me not just their time but something of themselves.

The lesson they taught me went deeper than a great deal of Exclusive Brethren teaching. Those children, bless them, led my faltering steps a little farther along the King's highway!

Chapter 12

VALLEY OF THE SHADOW

ON OUR FOURTH CHRISTMAS EVE together, Geoffrey cycled over to my parents to take them a present. He found my father seriously ill and my mother too bewildered to know what to do about it. Geoffrey immediately sent for the doctor. Soon afterwards an ambulance came to take my father to hospital. He died on Boxing Day, still a stranger to both of us. He always hated Christmas and died before finding out that it is a season of love and goodwill. His passing saddened me. He was so unloved in life and alone in death.

"If only he could have forgiven me for being born," I sobbed, "I'm sure I could have brought some sunshine and happiness to him, but he wouldn't let me."

"Regrets achieve nothing," Geoffrey said tenderly, taking me into his arms, but I knew his heart was touched with pity, too.

A year after my father's death my mother put her home up for sale. The house had four bedrooms and a large garden so she hoped to get a good price. A prospective buyer, whom I shall call Mr. Sharp, turned up immediately. After having gone thoroughly over the house, he brought his wife to see it. Suddenly he turned to my mother and asked to see the gas and electricity meters. Surprised, she showed him the cupboard under the stairs.

"I should turn these off at night," Mr. Sharp said. "I have three sons and don't wish any of them to commit suicide."

My mother, normally so phlegmatic, gaped at him. She could hardly wait to tell me about this softly-spoken house-hunter and his talk of suicide. She told me his name and that of his oldest son.

"Oh dear! I know that man," I exclaimed. "He's an Exclusive. Before I went to Brighton he asked me to marry him, but he was far too old for me. I didn't like him anyway."

My mother said I must be mistaken but I was quite certain. The talk of suicide made sense too. There had been one or two whispers of teenage suicides in the Exclusive Brethren that had been hushed up. Excessive study unbalancing the mind was rumoured to be the cause. I had my own opinions and suspected that these youngsters had been driven to take their own lives to escape from parental tyranny and the cruel system that enslaved them.

"It can't be the Mr. Sharp you know," my mother persisted. "I showed him your wedding photograph on the sideboard and he gave no sign of recognition."

"That's because I've left the Brethren. It's certainly the man who asked me to marry him," I replied, and told her where he lived and the name of his house. That convinced her.

Mr. Sharp had ready money, and because of this my mother was about to accept the reduced price he offered; but she was so incensed by his duplicity that she changed her mind.

"I can't see myself getting a fair deal from him," she said.

Years before I had felt sorry for Mr. Sharp's little boys, whose mother died when the youngest was born. I knitted them countless pullovers and sometimes took them out, but they were a job to handle. Their father had a succession of housekeepers, none of whom stayed long. This puzzled me because he seemed such a gentle, charming man. When I knew him better I discovered what a warped personality lay beneath the bland veneer. I was astonished too at the lack of discipline in his home. Most Brethren are rigid in their family domination, akin to Elizabeth's father in *The Barretts of Wimpole Street*. The first time I went to tea those spoiled little boys spat stones from the cherry jam all over the room, unchecked. No wonder the housekeepers could not face the job for long!

One evening, out of the blue, Mr. Sharp had asked me to marry him. I refused. No love existed between us and as a girl in my twenties I did not relish being unpaid housekeeper to a man approaching fifty who doted on and spoiled his children.

He later persuaded an older Sister to marry him. She was a smart business woman then, but it was pathetic to see how she declined after her marriage. With three unruly boys to cope with she had no time to think about her own appearance—not that an Exclusive husband would have encouraged her to look smart anyway.

When my mother saw her she could have mistaken her for a gypsy. Even her hair was unkempt, with a half-coiled bun falling down her back. My mother picked up several hair pins after she left.

"I reckon you had a lucky escape from that man," she said.

"Perhaps you have too," I laughed.

Shortly afterwards the house was sold at its full market value.

*   *   *   *

TWO MORE years passed, with their quota of work and play, happiness and regret. I was saddened by the disappearance of the lovely old house beyond the trees at the foot of our garden, but I forgot about it in the creativity of our holiday in Brixham. As mentioned earlier, Geoffrey had told me to write a book about a dying house. Then, typically, he helped me to write it. Work can be fun when two of you do it in harmony and that holiday proved deeply satisfying.

Geoffrey loved Brixham and I willingly agreed to return there the following summer. This time we did no work. We relaxed and enjoyed ourselves in glorious sunshine.

We returned home on a Saturday and the next day we went to an After Church Fellowship in a friend's house. These informal gatherings were very popular with the younger members of our church. We discussed topics of interest and exchanged views. Geoffrey never said much, but he loved the companionship and was a good listener.

This particular evening our host asked some of us to speak for a few minutes on our favourite Bible character. My mind was a complete blank at the time so I hoped he would not choose me; but he did. Oddly enough my mind was no longer blank. I felt compelled to speak about Joseph, how roughly his brothers treated him by throwing him into a pit, then, in jealous fury, selling him as a slave. Joseph had good cause to hate his brothers yet, when famine eventually reunited them, he showed a lovely spirit of forgiveness. I opened my Bible and read: "Be not grieved or angry with yourselves, for God sent me before you to preserve life." Again: "Ye meant it for evil, but God meant it for good."

I said that all of us have our trials to face. Others treat us badly and let us down. None of us knows what will happen tomorrow, but some problem may overwhelm us. God is concerned with our reaction to life's knocks. Will we have Joseph's forgiving spirit if someone wrongs us? What if grief or tragedy strike? Will we cry "Why me?" in hurt tones, or will we accept it as allowed by God for our ultimate good? I reminded the group that we all have to face trials sooner or later. We will either go through them with God, showing Joseph's gracious spirit, or we will be vindictive, rebellious and resentful.

I little dreamed how soon or how severely God would test me. Two days later Geoffrey went into hospital. He was to have an ingrown tooth removed from the roof of his mouth the next morning. He went to London for his "operation", as he jokingly called it, but did not want me to go with him. He smiled and waved to me as the train pulled out of the station.

I never saw him again.

The next morning a police car pulled up outside our maisonette and an officer rang at the door. Receiving no reply he asked a neighbour if she knew where I was. She directed him to my mother, who lived nearby. She told the policeman that I was working at *Punch*. Months later she told me that she wondered all day why the police had wanted me. It did not occur to her to ask! Neither did it occur to her to telephone and tell me that the police were looking for me. Had she done so it would have prepared me for the greatest shock of my life. Not that I blame her. She was not deliberately thoughtless. Anything out of the ordinary bewildered her and she "switched off".

When the hospital eventually contacted me at *Punch* to tell me that Geoffrey had died I could not take it in.

"You can't mean my husband," I gasped. "He's young and is only having a tooth out."

Of course it could not be my husband! Terrible things like that happen only to other people. Slowly the dreadful truth dawned. Horror changed to grief and grief threatened to give way to despair.

The days that followed are a blurred nightmare of the mortuary, the Coroner's Court and the office of the Registrar of Deaths. That Registrar was the one bright star that shone through the darkness. He told me to take up something creative as soon as possible.

"I can imagine you as a writer," he said. Bless his heart, it was a small thread to cling to—a gleam of purpose for my life.

Friends were marvellous and did all they could to help. Letters of sympathy arrived from far and near. I was particularly touched one day when I ran into dear old Mrs. Crouch, who used to clean for me.

"Cor lumme, what's 'appened to you, luv? You've gorn that thin," she said.

When I told her about Geoffrey the tears ran down her cheeks.

"Oh you poor dear," she sobbed, "and yer 'usband such a gent!"

She toddled off wiping her eyes, repeating "and 'im such a gent" as she went. Hers was the kind of sympathy that meant most to me.

Then there were the funeral flowers. Beautiful wreaths and sprays were piled on the cars. I was too dazed to take in much of the service but later, when all was quiet, I slipped back to the cemetery and took the little labels off those lovely flowers. I treasure them still. How kind people were!

It would all have been very different had Geoffrey's been an Exclusive funeral. No flowers would have adorned his coffin, flowers being worldly and part of fallen creation. (Since I left the Brethren I understand that flowers are no longer permitted in Brethren homes for the same reason.) Amid all the heartbreak an inner voice reminded me of my recent words —what if grief or tragedy strike? They had struck. Could I accept it as allowed by God for my good? Could I display Joseph's lovely spirit, or would I turn rebellious and resentful? I was deeply conscious that the group to whom I spoke would be looking at me now. What would they see?

Several of the young people did in fact ask: "Do you remember what you spoke about that Sunday before Geoff died? It was as if you were inspired. How could you foresee that God would test you like this?"

Yes, God was testing, testing to the utmost, and I tried to believe that what seemed so evil must be meant by Him for my ultimate good.

It was remarkable how God's words to Joshua came to me: "I will be with thee, I will not fail thee nor forsake thee . . . Be strong and of a good courage." Those words embedded themselves into my heart and mind and I could not escape them . . . "Be thou strong and very courageous. Have not I commanded thee, be strong . . . be not afraid, be not dismayed for the Lord thy God is with thee whithersoever thou goest."

On the way to the cemetery these same words ran through my mind, strengthening and comforting through the numbness.

I needed them all the time to lean on and act on, but it was easier said than done. I went through a terribly dark patch after the funeral. One night in particular stands out in my memory. At first I was too distressed to pray or even cry. I could only lie sleepless with a throbbing head. When I did cry to God the same words repeated themselves, almost as if they were spoken aloud. In my anguish I put my fingers in my ears to try to blot them out: "Have not I commanded thee? Be strong and of a good courage. Be not afraid, be not dismayed."

God seemed to wrestle with me that night and when morning dawned I was exhausted and at last the tears flowed. I was angry with God. Hurt that He had nothing else to say to me when I was in such a plight.

The postman brought an extra big batch of letters that morning. I crawled wearily down to get them. Only one letter mattered that day. It was the first one I opened and was from Geoffrey's brother Michael. He was a captain in the regular army, a man of few words, but when he spoke he expected to be obeyed. His letter was typical, only a few words, but to the point: "Have courage, Christine. Be steadfast."

Reading that, I came to the end of myself. I had battled with God over these very words all night, telling Him that they were no use, that they did not meet my need. Yet still He would not let me escape them! I admitted defeat, falling on my knees by the bed.

"Look, Lord, I am afraid," I said. "When I think of the future I'm scared stiff. I'm not strong either and, dear God, you've only to look at me to see I'm desperately dismayed. Why keep on saying the same thing to me?"

I reached for my Bible and some inner compulsion made me turn to the very verses I dreaded, almost hated. All in a flash realisation burst upon me. I had not listened properly, not heard completely. Now the full message leaped out from the page: "The Lord thy God is with thee whithersoever thou goest. . . . I will never leave thee nor forsake thee . . . . I will not fail thee."

How blind I had been! I had seen only my side, what I had to do, how I could cope. If only I had stopped struggling—let go and let God. He wanted to take away my fear. He wanted to make me strong, even perhaps a testimony to His enabling, but I would not let Him. He longed to comfort, but I was too immersed in self-pity for Him to get through to me. All night He had tried to tell me "I'm here. I'm holding you, I'll never let you go," and I had not listened.

Wonderful peace came as I handed myself over to God, grief, fright, weakness and all. It was a unique experience. In that moment I knew for certain that God is all powerful, even death has been conquered by His Son. I knew, too, that Geoffrey was not engulfed by death. It was but an horizon that he had passed beyond. He was out of my view, but alive in the presence of God.

In days to come several people were to ask how I could be so sure that there is a life after-death. I cannot give any tangible proof, who can?—but I *know* there is. Call it spiritual perception or what you will, but I just *know*. And I first knew experimentally, and not merely as a comfortable theory, in that moment when I handed myself over to God.

There beside the bed a warm, assuring glow flowed through me. It is hard to put into words, but God's love, power and peace enfolded me when I let them. I knew then, not only that Geoffrey had gone to be in God's presence, but that God was also very near to me. He would never leave me. He loved me too dearly. Wonderful revelation!

That evening a friend called unexpectedly. She worked in London but lived beyond Guildford. She kindly broke her journey to do what she could to help and comfort.

"When you opened the door I could tell you didn't need comforting," she said. "I was amazed by the radiant glow about you."

All I can say is that it was God's power still at work. The warmth with which He had filled me shone through for her to see.

I still love the story of Joseph and admire his attitude to adversity, saying to his brothers "You meant it for evil but God meant it for good." But experience humbles and I approach the story more cautiously now. Joseph was a spiritual giant beside whom I feel a pigmy. Nowadays I weigh my words carefully when I talk about how we should face our troubles.

Chapter 13

THE DEMON DOUBT

HOW EASY TO IMAGINE, because of God's loving dealing with me, that I would painlessly overcome further grief! But it was not so. The discovery quickly came that I still had to pass through a lonely valley with dark, depressing shadows.

One specially black day I turned to *The Christian's Secret of a Happy Life,* which Mrs. Hammond had given me in Brighton. On the fly-leaf she had written "Victory is experienced by a once-for-all abandonment of self to Christ, and a moment-by-moment, day-by-day trusting Him to hold control." I re-read those words many times. In happier days it had been so easy to talk of faith in overall terms, and to speak of trusting Him in a general way. Now believing and trusting were vital to every step of the way.

> *The soft sweet summer was warm and glowing,*
> *Bright were the blossoms on every bough;*
> *I trusted Him when the roses were blowing,*
> *I trust Him now.*

How pregnant with meaning Hannah Pearsall Smith's words had become. How precious too! I learned them by heart and they strengthened me.

A dreadful "cut off" feeling is one of the worst things you have to face when someone you love dies young. It seemed that Geoffrey's life had been snapped in half. He had so many plans, so many dreams for the future, so much potential. Even in the most everyday things this "cutting off" faced me. Before we went to Devon for that last holiday, he had begun to re-decorate the kitchen, a job that was badly overdue. He had time to do only the ceiling, and its gleaming whiteness made the badly distempered walls look a worse mess than ever. But now he had gone, and the job remained unfinished.

Sometimes I brooded over the plans that he had made—the country bungalow he would buy when he retired, the brick wall he would build round the garden, the rockery he would make, the waterfall . . . all dreams that would never come true. It was heart-breaking—and foolish to dwell upon.

One day I went to the Social Security Office to see about my Widow's Allowance. The lady who attended to me was a widow herself and could not have been kinder.

"I've been through it, my dear, and know what it's like," she sympathised, "but remember, you've got to make something of your life. Your husband would have wanted you to do that. You must make something of your life."

I stumbled out and sat by the Thames feeling deeply ashamed. What sort of testimony had I become to a living faith in God Who allows all for our good when I let the tears run down my face before that woman? I tried to justify myself on the grounds that the future looked so dark, bleak and empty. In silent prayer I turned to God for help. As I prayed His peace returned to my heart and I realised the future would not be dark if I walked with Him, and if I lived a day at a time. On that seat by the river I resolved, with God's help, to be courageous *today,* optimistic and useful *today.* It dawned on me, far more slowly than it should have done, that God promises us strength only for a day at a time. Here was I wearing myself out trying to carry tomorrow's load, and next week's load as well.

Material things like unpaid bills worried me. Not just those in my handbag, but those that would arrive next week, next month. How would they be paid? Here Geoffrey's practical example helped. I must *do* something about them.

The bills were paid in the end because I went back to full-time work to earn the money. I did not feel equal to a full day's work but took this job on the advice of a friend. Dorothy told me bluntly that I had too much time to feel sorry for myself and it spurred me into action. Money apart, when I look back I am grateful to her for encouraging me to take that job. With it came the discovery that doing something constructive is far less energy-sapping than self-pity.

Whenever I forgot to live a day at a time, the future held at least one dread. Fear of holidays was one of them. How could a holiday ever be enjoyable again? What sort of a farce would it be? Here another friend, Rosina, took things in hand. She invited me to go away with her. The prospect disinterested me so much that I did not even ask her where she was going. Like a good friend, Rosina arranged everything, booking for us both and paying the deposit. All I had to do was pack my case at the last minute and meet her at Waterloo Station. We had a splendid holiday!

I shall never forget the two baby mice in the drive of the guest house where we stayed. They were so busy licking an icecream paper that they did not mind a bit when I crouched down to watch them. One licked away delicately but the greedy one got his nose and tiny whiskers covered in ice cream and had to sit up and wash himself. I remember those little mice with gratitude. They taught me to laugh again.

One of the things I appreciated most after Geoffrey's death was the way my friends in the church invited me to their homes. I was helping one young wife with the washing up when she turned to me and said: "I can't understand how you can be so tranquil over Geoff's death. If my husband died like that I would hate God for it and take it out on Him. I couldn't believe He loved me if He let something so dreadful happen."

I had to do some quick heart-searching before replying. I tried to share with Jenny what I was still learning the hard way.

"You know, Jesus never promises His followers a bed of roses once they put their trust in Him," I said. "If we look upon Christianity as a kind of policy to ensure that everything will go right in our lives, then we'll be in for a big let-down. You've only to read of the beatings, hunger, imprisonment and martyrdom of the early Christians in Acts to realise that Christ hasn't promised His followers a smooth pathway."

"It's easy to *say* that," she murmured, and how right she was compared to believing it.

I told Jenny about *The Christian's Secret of a Happy Life* and how much it had helped me. "I specially love the poem at the end," I said:

> Small were my faith should it weakly falter
>   Now that the roses have ceased to blow;
> Frail were the trust that now should alter,
>   Doubting His love when the storm-clouds grow.

EXCLUSIVE BY-PATH

If I trust Him once I must trust Him ever,
And His way is best, though I stand or fall,
Through wind or storm He will leave me never,
For He sends all.

"I'm living with this poem," I said, "and I've asked myself why does 'He send all', including the storms of life? Surely it's because He doesn't want us to be fair-weather Christians. I've realised He wants me to be like the Apostle Paul, strong and courageous on stormy as well as sunny days, but it isn't easy."

"I think you're ever so brave," Jenny exclaimed.

"Not really," I confessed. "You're seeing me on a good day. I will say this though, I am proving Christ *is* sufficient for my need. How could I prove Him like this if the need wasn't there?"

Jenny looked sadly thoughtful and I wanted to hug her. She had not been married long and it was easy to see that losing her beloved Mike would be far too big a cross to bear. But then God is so loving and merciful that He does not ask any of us to bear something too great for us. He leads us gently, step by step, along His highway and He won't rush us to any milestone too quickly. Neither will He let any burden crush us when we do get there.

*   *   *   *

FOR SEVERAL months after Geoffrey's death, doubt was one of the worst demons that haunted me: Why did he die so young? Was it really God's will? Why did He allow it? Is He powerless to prevent tragedies? These are weighty questions calculated to undermine one's faith. I could not give a ready answer, only cling to God's promise that "All things work together for good to those who love Him." My other antidote to gnawing doubts was work. This proved an effective remedy for doubt's twin brother depression, too. I was too drained to take on the big jobs like decorating, but I tackled smaller tasks that would keep me occupied without becoming too exhausted.

One dreary Saturday I cleaned the kitchen cupboards. There was no need to hurry over it. Done leisurely it would keep me busy for quite a while. On the top shelf of the first cupboard I found two little plates. As I looked at them they took me back to that last holiday Geoffrey and I enjoyed in Brixham. I re-lived the lovely day we motored over the moors. After picnicking and basking in the sun, we went on to Widecombe. To my delight I discovered in a tiny shop a type of Devon pottery that was hard to find. Two of the small potteries that once made it had closed and the third had turned to new designs.

My landlord in Brighton first introduced me to this pottery when he gave me a coffee pot. It was brown on the inside, cream on the outside and inscribed with the words: "Do not stain today's blue skies with tomorrow's clouds." Wise words that I failed to heed! Afterwards I collected various pieces of this pottery: a cheese dish that tells me "Time and tide wait for no man", and a milk jug which lets me into the secret that "Fairest gems lie deepest", and so on.

At Widecombe I found a pile of little brown and cream plates each with a message round the rim. Geoffrey knew of the scarcity and told me to buy as many as I wanted. I chose six and we put them carefully in the car. We drove on and Geoffrey next parked near the river Dart. We strolled along the bank hand in hand, watching the trout in the crystal water . . . we crossed some stepping stones . . . glimpsed a kingfisher darting past . . . we watched a yellow wagtail, slender and long-legged, busy among the stones at the water's edge . . . we wandered towards a little tea room beside the river, where roses bloomed in abundance on a tumble-down trellis. . . .

> *The soft sweet summer was warm and glowing*
> *Bright were the blossoms on every bough.*
> *I trusted Him when the roses were blowing,*
> *I trust Him now.*

Tears filled my eyes as memory sharpened, blurring the words on the little plates in my hands. I recalled my surprise when we returned to our holiday flat and I unwrapped them. One said: "I'm not greedy but I like a". I stared in unbelief. How could I have bought a plate with an incomplete message? Geoffrey looked at it and suggested that we should take it back. This was as good an excuse as any for another visit to Dartmoor, so a few days later we had another picnic, then went on to Widecombe. We were just going into the shop when I had an idea.

"Let's keep this plate," I said.

Marriage had taught Geoffrey that women are apt to change their minds, so he looked at me in only mild surprise.

"It's essential to have one with the complete words as well, so we'll go in," I said.

Puzzled, he followed me into the shop. At the bottom of the pile I found what I wanted—another little plate saying "I'm not greedy but I like a lot."

Geoffrey asked why I wanted to keep the faulty plate.

I explained that the two would make a good object lesson for my Sunday Bible Class. I would ask the children if they finished things they started, or whether they grew tired and gave up. Even grown-ups sometimes leave jobs unfinished, I would tell them. Then I would hold up first the unfinished plate, then the other and get them to tell me which was the kind of workmanship that God wanted.

"I'll ask the children what they think happened to the man who made the first plate. Why didn't he finish it? Did someone interrupt him? Did his mind wander on to what he would have for dinner, or what he would do when he got home?"

"Isn't it strange that it got into the furnace incomplete?" Geoffrey said. "It's a permanent testimony to the fact that its maker did not complete his task."

While I was cleaning the kitchen cupboard I remembered what Geoffrey had said, and thought of the kind of man he was. The verse I had taught the children in my class came back to me: "Study to show thyself approved of God, a workman that needeth not to be ashamed." It described Geoffrey perfectly. As I fingered the little plate saying: "I'm not greedy but I like a" it pleased me to know that he would never have made a plate like that.

But it was the other plate that spoke to me that day. This one was complete. It reminded me that God is a Perfect Workman. Death could not thwart the sanctifying work that His Spirit had begun in Geoffrey's life—the work He begins in all our lives when we turn to Christ for salvation. Why was I so slow to grasp the truth? Death is no victor. It is but a horizon that takes our loved ones beyond the limit of our sight. God has them in His perfect care.

I must many times have read the verse "He Who has begun a good work in you will complete it until the day of Jesus Christ" without its full import coming home to me. Now those words *lived,* and I thrilled to the triumph of them. The Holy Spirit *will* complete what He has begun, and physical death—at whatever age—has no power to prevent it. One day every believer will be presented faultless in God's presence with exceeding joy.

I could not tell why Geoffrey should die so young, but it comforted me to realise that his death had not taken God by surprise. I could safely trust all to Him—and trust calmed my troubled spirit. Something, too, of the rapture of that glorious coming day gripped me, lifting me out of the Slough of Despond into which I had slipped.

The new message of those little plates filled my whole being with sunshine. I washed them carefully, then put them where I could see them. They serve to remind me that God is a Perfect Workman Who finishes what He begins, and His ways are perfect too.

Chapter 14

THE SUN BEYOND THE VALLEY

TRY AS I WOULD to banish them, haunting questions still lurked in my mind. Sometimes the physical aspect of Geoffrey's death troubled me. Why should a fit, strong man die while having a tooth out? Why had God allowed him to have an ingrown tooth anyway? This seemed specially ironical as Geoffrey's father had been a dentist and should have dealt with it years before.

Doubts—one of the devil's most successful weapons and one of the oldest too. He's been using Doubt ever since he put one in Eve's mind—"Did God say . . . ?"

The most persistent question was WHY? I often brooded over what I had been told at the Coroner's Court and tried to understand it. Geoffrey had, it appeared, died through excessive adrenalin in his bloodstream while under the anaesthetic. It stopped his heart, costing him his life. I remembered that it is fear which sends adrenalin into the bloodstream, but it never really made sense. When I recalled Geoffrey's cheery wave and smiling face as he left me, it was hard to believe.

One day I pondered these things while tidying the bookcase. Out fell a book by Dr. Vincent Peale entitled *The Amazing Results of Positive Thinking*. I had never read it and idly turned the pages. Suddenly a sentence arrested me and I read on. It is my belief that God intended me to read that page. It gave me an answer to many nagging questions:

I have been impressed many times by the effect of positive thinking on health and how dark negative thoughts tend to induce illness. Holding negative thoughts is very dangerous. Job said "The thing I greatly feared is come upon me." And Job was not the last to find that you can bring catastrophe upon yourself by unhealthy thinking.

Occasionally one comes across some dramatically eloquent example of this fact. In England I read a story in the London Daily Mail *describing the curious death of Gem Gilbert, a British tennis star. She had died as a dentist was about to extract a tooth.*

Years before, when Gem Gilbert was a small girl, she had gone to the dentist where her mother was to have a tooth out. And a most unusual and tragic thing happened. The little girl, terrified, watched her mother die in the dentist's chair. So what happened? Her mind painted an indelible picture of herself dying in the same way. The picture became a mental reality. Gem Gilbert carried it in her mind for thirty years. This fear was so real that she would never go to a dentist, no matter how badly she needed treatment.

But finally there came a time when she was suffering such acute pain that she agreed to have a dentist come to her house to extract a tooth. . . . She sat in the chair. The dentist put a bib around her. He took out his instruments and at the sight of them—she died.

The writer in the Daily Mail *remarked that Gem Gilbert had been killed by "thirty years of thought".*

The book slipped from my fingers. Tears coursed down my cheeks, but at last I understood. I had known for years that my husband was terrified of injections and had warned both our doctor and dentist of this, since Geoffrey fainted at the sight of a hypodermic syringe. What I did not know was the deep underlying cause of this fear. Nor did I know how far-reaching was his dread of anything that could make him unconscious.

Geoffrey rarely spoke of his childhood but reading about Gem Gilbert instantly brought the major event of his early years to my mind. One sunny day his father took him to play on the beach. When they returned home Geoffrey ran indoors to tell Mummy all about it. He flung open the kitchen door and found his mother lying with her head in the gas oven. The next minute his father grabbed him and threw him into the garden. He had scarcely picked himself up before his father stumbled out with his mother in his arms. He laid her on the grass and tried in vain to revive her, while Geoffrey stood by screaming. . . . The police arrived. . . . An ambulance took his mother away. . . . Horrified neighbours whispered "She's gassed herself"—and terror struck at the heart of a little six-years-old boy.

For more than thirty years Geoffrey must have nursed a secret dread of anything that could render him unconscious. If it did, would not he too die?

When I thought of the cheery way he waved to me I realised how brave he was. If only I could have gone to that hospital with him—put my arms round him. . . .

But doubts departed with the coming of greater understanding as I read Dr. Vincent Peale's book. I rejoiced that God knew *all* the circumstances and had taken Geoffrey to be with Himself, where all is light and love and where he would never know fear again.

*   *   *   *

A YEAR after Geoffrey died the young people at our church arranged a house-party at Greenhills, Worthing.

Mrs. Hitchcock, the minister's wife, tried to persuade me to go. I excused myself on the grounds that I was not in the right age group. In fact I was very tired and had many things on my mind. A week-end surrounded by noisy teenagers seemed more than I could cope with. Mrs. Hitchcock insisted, saying that the change would do me good. Eventually I relented and was grateful for her thoughtfulness in giving me a room to myself.

On the Saturday morning I met Douglas, a late arrival, in the hall. Immediately my mind flashed back eighteen months to the first time we had met. This was at the same Conference Centre with the same crowd of young people, except that Geoffrey had been with us then. Officially we were too old, being in our late thirties, but the young people had asked my husband to be House-party Treasurer. He had willingly agreed, and covered our bed with the fees he collected! Meticulous as always, he had not been happy until every penny balanced and all outpayments were settled.

On that occasion our minister had told us that his cousin, Douglas Wood, was coming from Brighton for part of the time and asked Geoffrey to arrange with him about reduced fees. When he arrived, Geoffrey went downstairs to see "the chap who shared his surname". He was gone a long time. Eventually I went to investigate and found him and Douglas deep in conversation. I thought how nice they looked standing there together, both in grey trousers and white shirts. We were pleased to meet Douglas because he was the only other guest in his thirties.

Now, here he was again and we re-introduced ourselves. He suggested a walk and we went to the pier to watch some anglers.

"Look, that one's caught a tadpole!" Douglas exclaimed.

We laughed as we watched the man winding in a small piece of bladderwrack seaweed, and felt completely at ease in each other's company.

That afternoon I discovered that life had had its ups and downs for Douglas and realised that widows do not have a monopoly of loneliness. Bachelors have their share as the years advance, and Douglas had all but given up hope of meeting the one woman who would give him her love, understanding and companionship.

Before we parted Douglas confided that he had not wanted to come to Worthing that week-end, but was glad that he had yielded to his cousin's persuasion. We both knew that a firm link had been forged in friendship's chain.

It pleased me when I later heard that Douglas was leaving Brighton to live in Surrey. Friendship would be easier to give—and receive—at closer range.

So I set out eagerly towards yet another milestone—beyond the Valley of the Shadow. My step was light and I had a song, yes a song, in my heart:

Music from the homeland fills me with delight,
Walking in the King's highway;
Visions of the glory break upon my sight,
Walking in the King's highway.

Crowned with tender mercies, guarded by His love,
Walking in the King's highway;
Jesus gives a foretaste of the joys above,
Walking in the King's highway.